The Big Book
of
7,000
Unique Baby Names
(With Origins and Meanings)

Laura Weaver

Table of Contents

Africa

For someone looking to add a name that won't easily be found on keychains, or to give your new baby a name full of tradition and promise, think African baby names. African baby names (which include Muslim, Christian, Jewish and Arabic origin names) are beautiful, exotic, and full of deeper meaning. You also probably won't find anyone else with these names, especially in traditional classrooms. Some famous examples of African baby names include Barack (Swahili for "blessing") or Aaliyah (meaning "to rise up").

Name	Meaning	Origin
Aba	Born on Thursday	Fante, Ghana
Ababuo	A child that keeps coming back	Ewe, Ghana
Abagbe	We begged to have this one to lift up	Yoruba, Nigeria
Abam	Second child after twins	Twi, Ghana
Abayomi	She brings joy	Yoruba, Nigeria
Abebi	We asked for her	Yoruba, Nigeria
Abeje	We asked to have this child	Yoruba, Nigeria
Abeke	We asked for her to pet her.	Yoruba, Nigeria
Abena	Born on Tuesday	Fante, Ghana
Abeni	We asked for her	Yoruba, Nigeria
Abeo	Her birth brings happiness	Yoruba, Nigeria
Abidemi	Born during the father's absence	Yoruba, Nigeria
Abikanile	Listen	Yao, Malawi

Abimbola	Born to be wealthy	Yoruba, Nigeria
Abiona	Born on a journey	Yoruba, Nigeria
Adamma	Child of beauty	Ibo, Nigeria
Adebola	Honor is hers	Yoruba, Nigeria
Adedagbo	Happiness is a crown	Yoruba, Nigeria
Adeleka	Crown brings happiness	Yoruba, Nigeria
Adelola	Crown brings honor	Yoruba, Nigeria
Adesimbo	Noble birth	Yoruba, Nigeria
Adesina	This child opens the way	Yoruba, Nigeria
Adia	Present of God	Swahili, East Africa
Adowa	Born on Tuesday	Akan, Ghana
Aduke	Beloved, cherished	Yoruba, Nigeria
Afafa	The first child of the second husband	Ewe, Ghana
Afiya	Health	Swahili, East Africa
Afryea	Born during happy times	Ewe, Ghana
Afua	Born on Friday	Ewe, Ghana
Aina	Difficult birth	Yoruba, Nigeria
Aisha	Life	Swahili, East Africa
Aiyetoro	Peace on earth	Yoruba, Nigeria
Akanke	To know her is to love her	Yoruba, Nigeria
Akilah	Intelligent	Arabic, North Africa
Akosua	Born on Sunday	Ewe, Ghana
Akua	Born on Wednesday	Ewe, Ghana
Akwete	First born of twins	Ga, Ghana
Akwokwo	Younger of twins	Ga, Ghana

Alaba	Second child born after twins	Yoruba, Nigeria
Alake	One to be petted and fussed over	Yoruba, Nigeria
Alile	She weeps	Yao, Malawi
Aluna	Come here	Mwera, Kenya
Ama	Born on Saturday	Ewe, Ghana
Amadi	Rejoicing	Ibo, Nigeria
Aminah	Trustworthy	Swahili, East Africa
Asabi	She is of choice birth	Yoruba, Nigeria
Asha	To live	Swahili, East Africa
Asya	Born during a time of grief	Swahili, East Africa
Ayobami	I am blessed with you	Yoruba, Nigeria
Ayobunmi	Joy is given to me	Yoruba, Nigeria
Ayodele	Joy comes home	Yoruba, Nigeria
Ayofemi	Joy likes me	Yoruba, Nigeria
Ayoluwa	Joy of the people	Yoruba, Nigeria
Ayoola	Joy is wealth	Yoruba, Nigeria
Aziza	Precious	Swahili, East Africa
Baako	First born	Akan, Ghana
Baba	Born on Thursday	Fante, Ghana
Baderinwa	Worthy of respect	Yoruba, Nigeria
Bahati	My luck is good	Swahili, East Africa
Barika	Successful	Yoruba, Nigeria
Bayo	Joy is found	Yoruba, Nigeria
Bejide	Born during a rainy season	Yoruba, Nigeria
Bolade	Honor arrives	Yoruba, Nigeria
Bolanile	Wealth of this	Yoruba, Nigeria

	house	
Bunmi	My gift	Yoruba, Nigeria
Buseje	Ask me	Yao, Malawi
Chaonaine	It has seen me	Ngoni, Malawi
Chausiki	Born at night	Swahili, East Africa
Chiku	Chatter box	Swahili, East Africa
Chinue	Blessing of Chi	Ibo, Nigeria
Chipo	Gift	Shona, Zimbabwe
Chuki	Born during a time of hatred	Swahili, East Africa
Dada	Child with curly hair	Yoruba, Nigeria
Dalila	Gentle soul	Swahili, East Africa
Dalili	Sign, omen	Swahili, East Africa
Dayo	Joy arrives	Yoruba, Nigeria
Do	First child after twins	Ewe, Ghana
Dofi	Second child born after twins	Ewe, Ghana
Doto	Second of twins	Zaramo, Tanzania
Dziko	The world	Nguni, South Africa
Ebun	Gift	Yoruba, Nigeria
Efia	Born on Friday	Fante, Ghana
Enomwoyi	Graceful one	Benin, Nigeria
Enyonyam	It is good for me	Ewe, Ghana
Eshe	Life	Swahili, East Africa
Esi	Born on Sunday	Fante, Ghana
Fabayo	A lucky birth brings joy	Yoruba, Nigeria
Faizah	Victorious	Arabic, North Africa
Fayola	Walk with honor	Yoruba, Nigeria
Femi	Love me	Yoruba, Nigeria
Fola	Honorable	Yoruba, Nigeria
Folade	She brings honor	Yoruba, Nigeria
Folami	Honor and respect me	Yoruba, Nigeria
Folayan	To walk with dignity	Yoruba, Nigeria

Foluke	Placed in God's care	Yoruba, Nigeria
Fujo	Born after a quarrel	Swahili, East Africa
Fukayna	Knowledgeable	Egyptian, North Africa
Habiba	Sweetheart	Swahili, East Africa
Hadiya	Guide	Swahili, East Africa
Halima	Gentle, patient	Swahili, East Africa
Hanifa	True believer of Islam	Arabic, North Africa
Hasanati	Good	Swahili, East Africa
Hasina	Good	Swahili, East Africa
Hawa	Eve	Swahili, East Africa
Hembadoon	The winner	Tiv, Nigeria
Husniya	Beauty	Arabic, North Africa
Idowu	First child after twins	Yoruba, Nigeria
Ifama	All is well	Ibo, Nigeria
Ife	Love	Yoruba, Nigeria
Ifetayo	Love brings happiness	Yoruba, Nigeria
Ikuseghan	Peace is better than war	Benin, Nigeria
Isoke	A wonderful gift from God	Benin, Nigeria
Iverem	Blessing and favor	Tiv, Nigeria
Izegbe	Long-awaited child	Benin, Nigeria
Jaha	Dignity	Swahili, East Africa
Jamila	Beautiful, elegant	Swahili, East Africa
Japera	Now we offer thanks	Shona, Zimbabwe
Jendayi	Give thanks	Shona, Zimbabwe
Jumoke	Everyone loves the child	Yoruba, Nigeria
Kakra	Second of twins	Fante, Ghana

Kamaria	Moonlight, like the moon	Swahili, East Africa
Kehinde	Second of twins	Yoruba, Nigeria
Kesi	Born when the father had troubles	Swahili, East Africa
Khadija	Born prematurely	Swahili, East Africa
Kibibi	Little lady	Swahili, East Africa
Kissa	Born after twins	Luganda, Uganda
Kokumo	This one will not die	Yoruba, Nigeria
Kukua	Born on Wednesday	Fante, Ghana
Kuliraga	Weeping	Yao, Malawi
Kulwa	First born of twins	Zaramo, Tanzania
Kunto	Third born child	Twi, Ghana
Kyalamboka	God save me	Nyakyusa, Tanzania
Lateefa	Gentle, kind	Arabic, North Africa
Lulu	A pearl	Swahili, East Africa
Lumusi	Born face downward	Ewe, Ghana
Mama	Born on Saturday	Fante, Ghana
Mandisa	Sweet	Xhosa, South Africa
Marjani	Coral	Swahili, East Africa
Mashavu	Cheeks	Swahili, East Africa
Mashika	Born during a rainy season	Swahili, East Africa
Mawiyah	The essence of life	Arabic, North Africa
Mawusi	In the hands of God	Ewe, Ghana
Mesi	Water	Yao, Malawi
Monifa	I am lucky	Yoruba, Nigeria
Morowa	Queen	Akan, Ghana
Mosi	First born	Swahili, East Africa

Mudiwa	Beloved, dearest	Shona, Zimbabwe
Muminah	Pious woman	Arabic, North Africa
Munirah	Enlightened woman	Arabic, North Africa
Mwanawa	First born	Zaramo, Tanzania
Nabulungi	Beautiful one	Luganda, Uganda
Naeemah	To be carefree	Arabic, North Africa
Nailah	One who succeeds	Arabic, North Africa
Namono	Younger of twins	Luganda, Uganda
Nanyamka	God's gift	Ewe, Ghana
Nathifa	One who is pure	Arabic, North Africa
Nayo	She is our joy	Yoruba, Nigeria
Neema	Born during prosperous times	Swahili, East Africa
Nehanda	Strong and powerful	Zezuru, Zimbabwe
Ngabile	I have it	Nyakyusa, Tanzania
Ngozi	Blessing	Ibo, Nigeria
Njemile	Upstanding, honorable	Yao, Malawi
Nkosazana	Princess	Xhosa, South Africa
Nneka	Her mother is important	Ibo, Nigeria
Nomalanga	Sunny	Zulu, South Africa
Nombeko	Respect	Xhosa, South Africa
Nomble	Beauty	Xhosa, South Africa
Nomusa	Compassionate, merciful	Ndebele, Zimbabwe
Nourbese	Wonderful child	Benin, Nigeria
Nuru	To illuminate	Swahili, East Africa
Obioma	Kind woman	Ibo, Nigeria
Ode	Born along the road	Benin, Nigeria
Olabisi	Joy is multiplied	Yoruba, Nigeria
Olaniyi	There's glory in wealth	Yoruba, Nigeria

Olubayo	Greatest joy	Yoruba, Nigeria
Olufemi	God loves me	Yoruba, Nigeria
Olufunmilayo	God gives me joy	Yoruba, Nigeria
Oluremi	God consoles me	Yoruba, Nigeria
Omolara	Born at the right time	Benin, Nigeria
Omorose	Beautiful child	Benin, Nigeria
Omusupe	She is the most precious thing	Benin, Nigeria
Oni	Born in a sacred place	Yoruba, Nigeria
Oseye	Happy one	Benin, Nigeria
Panya	Mouse, reference to a small baby	Swahili, East Africa
Panyin	First born of twins	Fante, Ghana
Pasua	Born by cesarean section	Swahili, East Africa
Pili	Second born	Swahili, East Africa
Rabiah	Spring breeze	Arabic, North Africa
Radhiya	Agreeable	Swahili, East Africa
Ramila	Fortune teller	Swahili, East Africa
Rashida	Righteous	Swahili, East Africa
Raziya	Agreeable	Swahili, East Africa
Rehema	Compassionate	Swahili, East Africa
Rufaro	Happiness	Shona, Zimbabwe
Rukiya	Rising up	Swahili, East Africa
Saada	Helpful	Swahili, East Africa
Sabah	Morning	Arabic, North Africa
Safiya	Pure	Swahili, East Africa
Saidah	Fortunate	Arabic, North Africa
Salama	Peace	Swahili, East Africa
Salihah	Correct	Arabic, North Africa
Salma	Safe	Swahili, East Africa
Sanura	Intelligent,	Swahili, East Africa

	creative	
Sauda	Dark beauty	Swahili, East Africa
Sekelaga	Rejoice	Nyakyusa, Tanzania
Shani	Marvelous	Swahili, East Africa
Sharifa	Distinguished	Swahili, East Africa
Shukura	Grateful	Swahili, East Africa
Sibongile	Appreciation, Thanks	Ndebele, Zimbabwe
Sigele	Left	Ngoni, Malawi
Sisi	Born on Sunday	Fante, Ghana
Siti	Respected woman	Swahili, East Africa
Subira	Patience is rewarded	Swahili, East Africa
Suhailah	Gentle soul	Arabic, North Africa
Suma	Ask	Nyakyusa, Tanzania
Tabia	Gifted	Swahili, East Africa
Taiwo	First born of twins	Yoruba, Nigeria
Takiyah	Piety	Arabic, North Africa
Taliba	Seeker of knowledge	Arabic, North Africa
Teleza	Slippery	Ngoni, Malawi
Thandiwe	Affectionate	Xhosa, South Africa
Thema	Queen	Akan, Ghana
Themba	Trusted	Zulu, South Africa
Titilayo	Eternal happiness	Yoruba, Nigeria
Tulinagwe	God is with us	Nyakyusa, Tanzania
Tusajigwe	We are blessed	Nyakyusa, Tanzania
Uchenna	God's will	Ibo, Nigeria
Ulu	Second born female	Ibo, Nigeria
Umayma	Little mother	Arabic, North Africa
Umm	Mother	Arabic, North Africa
Urbi	Princess	Benin, Nigeria
Uwimana	Daughter of God	Rwanda, Rwanda
Walidah	Newborn	Arabic, North Africa

Waseme	Let them talk	Swahili, East Africa
aa	Born on Thursday	Ewe, Ghana
Yamina	Proper	Arabic, North Africa
Ye	First born of twins	Ewe, Ghana
Yejide	She looks like her mother	Yoruba, Nigeria
Zahara	Blossom	Swahili, East Africa
Zahra	Blossom	Swahili, East Africa
Zainabu	Fragrant plant	Swahili, East Africa
Zakiya	Pure	Swahili, East Africa
Zalika	Well-born	Swahili, East Africa
Zawadi	Gift	Swahili, East Africa
Zesiro	First born of twins	Luganda, Uganda
Zubaidah	Marigold	Arabic, North Africa
Zuwena	Good	Swahili, East Africa
BOYS	**MEANING**	**ORIGIN**
Abayomi	Born to bring me joy	Yoruba, Nigeria
Abdalla	Servant of God	Swahili, East Africa
Abdu	Worshiper of God	Swahili, East Africa
Abeeku	Born on Wednesday	Fante, Ghana
Abejide	Born during winter	Yoruba, Nigeria
Abiodun	Born at the time of war	Yoruba, Nigeria
Abiola	Born in honor	Yoruba, Nigeria
Addae	Morning sun	Akan, Ghana
Ade	Royal	Yoruba, Nigeria
Adebayo	He came in a joyful time	Yoruba, Nigeria
Adeben	Twelfth-born	Akan, Ghana
Adesola	The crown honored us	Yoruba, Nigeria

Adika	The first child of a second husband	Ewe, Ghana
Adio	Be righteous	Yoruba, Nigeria
Adisa	One who makes himself clear	Yoruba, Nigeria
Adofo	Warrior	Akan, Ghana
Adom	Help from God, God's blessing	Akan, Ghana
Adunbi	Born to be pleasant	Yoruba, Nigeria
Adusa	Thirteenth-born	Akan, Ghana
Ahmed	Praiseworthy	Swahili, East Africa
Ajani	The victor	Yoruba, Nigeria
Akanni	Our encounter brings possession	Yoruba, Nigeria
Akiiki	Friend	Muneyankole, Uganda
Akinlabi	We have a boy	Yoruba, Nigeria
Akinlana	Valor	Yoruba, Nigeria
Akins	Brave boy	Yoruba, Nigeria
Akono	It is my turn	Yoruba, Nigeria
Akwtee	Younger of twins	Ga, Ghana
Ali	Exalted	Swahili, East Africa
Amadi	He seems destined to die at birth	Benin, Nigeria
Anane	Fourth son	Akan, Ghana
Andwele	God brought me	Nyakyusa, Tanzania
Anum	Fifth-born	Akan, Ghana
Apara	A child that comes and goes	Yoruba, Nigeria
Asim	Protector	Swahili, East Africa
Aswad	Black	Arabic, North Africa
Atsu	Younger of twins	Ewe, Ghana
Atu	Born on Saturday	Fante, Ghana
Ayize	Let it happen	Zulu, South Africa

Ayo	Happiness	Yoruba, Nigeria
Azizi	Precious	Swahili, East Africa
Babafemi	My father loves me	Yoruba, Nigeria
Badru	Born between full moons	Swahili, East Africa
Bakari	Of noble promise	Swahili, East Africa
Baruti	Teacher	Tswana, Botswana
Bem	Peace	Tiv, Nigeria
Bobo	Born on Tuesday	Fante, Ghana
Bomani	Warrior	Ngoni, Malawi
Boseda	Born on Sunday	Tiv, Nigeria
Chenzira	Born on the road	Shona, Zimbabwe
Chijioke	God gives talent	Ibo, Nigeria
Chike	Power of God	Ibo, Nigeria
Chinelo	Thought of God	Ibo, Nigeria
Chinua	Blessings of God	Ibo, Nigeria
Chioke	God blessing	Ibo, Nigeria
Chiumbo	Small, small child, small creation	Mwera, Kenya
Dada	Curly hair	Yoruba, Nigeria
Dakarai	Happiness	Shona, Zimbabwe
Daudi	Beloved	Swahili, East Africa
Dawud	Beloved	Arabic, North Africa
Dulani	Cutting	Ngoni, Malawi
Dumaka	Helping hands	Ibo, Nigeria
Ebo	Born on Tuesday	Fante, Ghana
Ehioze	Jealousy is beneath me	Benin, Nigeria
Fadil	Generous	Arabic, North Africa
Fakih	One who recites the Koran	Arabic, North Africa
Faraji	Consolation	Swahili, East Africa
Fifi	Born on Friday	Fante, Ghana
Foluke	Given to God	Yoruba, Nigeria

Funsani	Request	Ngoni, Malawi
Gahiji	The hunter	Rwanda, Rwanda
Gamba	Warrior	Shona, Zimbabwe
Gowon	Rainmaker	Tiv, Nigeria
Gwandoya	Met with misery	Luganda, Uganda
Gyasi	Wonderful baby	Akan, Ghana
Habib	Beloved	Arabic, North Africa
Habimana	God exist	Rwanda, Rwanda
Haji	Born during the hajj	Swahili, East Africa
Hamadi	Praised	Swahili, East Africa
Hanif	True believer of Islam	Arabic, North Africa
Harith	Cultivator	Arabic, North Africa
Harun	Lofty	Arabic, North Africa
Hasani	Handsome	Swahili, East Africa
Hashim	Destroying	Arabic, North Africa
Hondo	Warrior	Shona, Zimbabwe
Ibrahim	Father of a multitude	Hausa, Nigeria
Idi	Born during the Idd festival	Swahili, East Africa
Imarogbe	Child born to a good and caring family	Benin, Nigeria
Ipyana	Grace	Nyakyusa, Tanzania
Ishaq	Laughter	Arabic, North Africa
Issa	Salvation	Swahili, East Africa
Iyapo	Many trials	Yoruba, Nigeria
Jabari	Comforter	Swahili, East Africa
Jabulani	Happy	Ndebele, Zimbabwe
Jafari	Stream	Swahili, East Africa
Jahi	Dignity	Swahili, East Africa
Jaja	Honored one	Ibo, Nigeria
Jela	The father is in prison at the time of birth	Swahili, East Africa
Jelani	Mighty	Ibo, Nigeria

Jojo	Born on Monday	Fante, Ghana
Juma	Born on Friday	Swahili, East Africa
Jumaane	Born on Tuesday	Swahili, East Africa
Jumoke	Loved by everyone	Yoruba, Nigeria
Kafele	Worth dying for	Ngoni, Malawi
Kamau	Quiet warrior	Kikuyu, Kenya
Kasiya	Departure	Ngoni, Malawi
Kayode	He brought joy	Yoruba, Nigeria
Kehinde	Second born of twins	Yoruba, Nigeria
Kereenyaga	Mountain of mystery	Kikuyu, Kenya
Khaldun	Eternal	Arabic, North Africa
Khalfani	Destined to lead	Swahili, East Africa
Khalid	Eternal	Arabic, North Africa
Khamisi	Born on Thursday	Swahili, East Africa
Kitwana	Pledged to live	Swahili, East Africa
Kizza	Born after twins	Luganda, Uganda
Kodwo	Born on Monday	Twi, Ghana
Kofi	Born on Friday	Twi, Ghana
Kojo	Born on Monday	Akan, Ghana
Kokayi	Summon the people	Shona, Zimbabwe
Kondo	War	Swahili, East Africa
Kontar	Only child	Akan, Ghana
Kosoko	No hoe to dig a grave	Yoruba, Nigeria
Kpodo	First born of twins	Ewe, Ghana
Kufuo	The father shared the pains of birth	Fante, Ghana
Kwabena	Born on Tuesday	Akan, Ghana
Kwakou	Born on Wednesday	Ewe, Ghana
Kwasi	Born on Sunday	Akan, Ghana

Kwayera	Dawn	Ngoni, Malawi
Lateef	Gentle	Arabic, North Africa
Lebna	Soul, spirit	Amharic and Tigrinya, Ethiopia
Lisimba	Hurt by a lion	Yao, Malawi
Lutalo	Warrior	Luganda, Uganda
Machupa	One who likes to drink	Swahili, East Africa
Madu	People	Ibo, Nigeria
Madzimoyo	Water of life	Ngoni, Malawi
Malawa	Blossoms, flowers	Yao, Malawi
Mandala	Spectacles	Ngoni, Malawi
Masamba	Leaves	Yao, Malawi
Masud	Fortunate	Swahili, East Africa
Mawuli	There is a God	Ewe, Ghana
Mazi	Sir	Ibo, Nigeria
Mensah	Third-born son	Ewe, Ghana
Mhina	Delightful	Swahili, East Africa
Mosi	Fifth-born	Swahili, East Africa
Munyiga	One who bothers other people	Mukiga, Uganda
Musa	Child	Swahili, East Africa
Mwamba	Powerful	Nyakyusa, Tanzania
Najja	Born after	Muganda, Uganda
Nakisisa	Child of the shadows	Muganda, Uganda
Nassor	Victorious	Swahili, East Africa
Ndale	A trick	Ngoni, Malawi
Ndulu	Dove	Tigrinya, Ethiopia
Ngozi	Good fortune	Ibo, Nigeria
Njau	Young bull	Kikuyu, Kenya
Nwabudike	The son is the father's power	Ibo, Nigeria
Obasi	In honor of the supreme God	Ibo, Nigeria

Obataiye	King of the world	Yoruba, Nigeria
Obayana	The king warms himself at the fire	Yoruba, Nigeria
Obi	Heart	Ibo, Nigeria
Obike	A strong household	Ibo, Nigeria
Odion	First born of twins	Ibo, Nigeria
Ogbonna	The image of his father	Ibo, Nigeria
Ojore	A man of war	Ateso, Uganda
Okechuku	A gift of God	Ibo, Nigeria
Okello	Born after twins	Ateso, Uganda
Okpara	Fifth-born son	Ibo, Nigeria
Oladele	We are honored at home	Yoruba, Nigeria
Olafemi	Honor favors me	Yoruba, Nigeria
Olaniyan	Surrounded by honor	Yoruba, Nigeria
Olubayo	Rejoicing	Yoruba, Nigeria
Olufemi	Wealth and honor favors me	Yoruba, Nigeria
Olugbala	Savior of the people	Yoruba, Nigeria
Olujimi	God has given me this	Yoruba, Nigeria
Olumide	God arrives	Yoruba, Nigeria
Olumiji	My lord awakens	Yoruba, Nigeria
Olushola	God has blessed me	Yoruba, Nigeria
Oluwa	Our lord	Yoruba, Nigeria
Oluyemi	Fulfillment from God, satisfied	Yoruba, Nigeria
Osakwe	God agrees	Benin, Nigeria
Osayimwese	God made me complete	Benin, Nigeria

Osei	Honorable, noble	Fante, Ghana
Paki	Witness	Xhosa, South Africa
Rafiki	Friend	Swahili, East Africa
Ranako	Handsome	Shona, Zimbabwe
Rashidi	Rightly guided	Swahili, East Africa
Rudo	Love	Shona, Zimbabwe
Sadiki	Faithful	Swahili, East Africa
Salehe	Good man	Swahili, East Africa
Salih	Righteous	Arabic, North Africa
Salim	Safe	Swahili, East Africa
Sefu	Sword	Swahili, East Africa
Sekayi	Laughter	Shona, Zimbabwe
Simba	Lion	Swahili, East Africa
Sulaiman	Peaceful	Arabic, North Africa
Tahir	Pure	Arabic, North Africa
Taiwo	First born of twins	Yoruba, Nigeria
Talib	Seeker	Arabic, North Africa
Tau	Lion	Tswana, Botswana
Thabiti	A man	Mwera, Kenya
Thandiwe	Beloved	Zulu, South Africa
Themba	Hope	Xhosa, South Africa
Tumaini	Hope	Mwera, Kenya
Uchechi	God's will	Ibo, Nigeria
Umi	Life	Yao, Malawi
Unika	To shine	Lomwe, Malawi
Useni	Tell me	Yao, Malawi
Walid	Newborn	Arabic, North Africa
Wambua	Born during the rainy season	Kamba, Kenya
Wekesa	Born during the harvest time	Lechya, Kenya
Yafeu	Bold	Fante, Ghana
Yazid	To become greater	Swahili, East Africa
Yonas	Dove	Ethiopia

Zahur	Flower	Swahili, East Africa
Zesiro	First born of twins	Buganda, Uganda
Zikomo	Thank you	Ngoni, Malawi
Ziyad	To become greater	Arabic, North Africa
Zuberi	Strong	Swahili, East Africa

Anglo Saxon

Anglo Saxon baby names are what most people would call "traditional names." These are the names that are deeply rooted in historical, literary, and pop culture. Some of these names come from Old English, meaning they can be difficult to pronounce or can be pronounced in different ways. Some of these names are more old fashioned, but they have a regality that cannot be paralleled by other names. Some popular examples include Avery (Elf ruler), Catherine (Pure), and Drew (manly).

GIRLS	MEANING	ORIGIN
Acca	Unity	Latin
Afra	Young doe	Hebrew
Afton	From Afton	English
Ainsley	My own meadow	Scottish
Aisly	Dwells at the ash tree meadow	Scottish
Alberta	Noble and bright	German
Alodia	Rich	Unknown
Alodie	Rich	Unknown
Althena	Healer	Greek
Amity	Friendship	Latin
Annis	Pure	English
Antonia	Priceless, inestimable or praiseworthy	Latin
Ara	Opinionated	Arabic
Ardith	Flowering field	Hebrew

Arleigh	Meadow of the hare	Old English
Arlette	Pledge	Old English
Ashley	Meadow of ash trees	Old English
Audrey	Noble strength	Old English
Augusta	Venerable	Latin
Beatrix	She who brings happiness	German
Becky	Bound	American
Berenice	She will bring victory	Greek
Bliss	Delight joy or happiness	Old English
Blythe	Cheerful	Old English
Bonnie	Pretty	English
Breck	Freckled	Irish
Bree	Strong	Irish
Bridget	Strength	Irish
Brimlad	Seaway	Unknown
Britt	From Britian	Old English
Cate	Pure	Greek
Catherine	Pure	Greek
Catheryn	Pure	Greek
Cathryn	Pure	Greek
Chelsea	Port or landing place	Old English
Clover	Clover	Old English
Constance	Constant or steadfast	Latin
Coventina	Water Goddess	Greek
Cwen	Queen	Welsh
Cwene	Queen	Welsh
Daisy	Eye of the day	Old English
Darel	Darling or beloved	French
Darelene	Darling	French
Darelle	Darling or beloved	French
Darlene	Darling	French
Darline	Darling	French
Daryl	Darling	French
Dawn	Daybreak or sunrise	English
Devona	From Devonshire	English
Diera	From Diera	Unknown
Dolly	Gift of God	American

Domino	Belonging to the Lord	English
Doretta	Gift of God	English
Doris	Of the sea	Greek
Eadlin	Princess	Unknown
Earlene	Noblewoman	English
Eartha	Earthy	English
Easter	Born at Easter	English
Eda	Wealthy	English
Edina	Ardent	Irish
Edit	Prosperous in war	Old English
Edita	Prosperous in war	Spanish
Edith	Prosperous in war	Old English
Editha	Prosperous in war	German
Edla	Princess	Unknown
Edlin	Princess	English
Edwina	Prosperous friend	Old English
Edyt	Prosperous in war	Old English
Edyth	Prosperous in war	Old English
Elda	Old and wise protector	Old English
Elene	Light	Greek
Elga	Pious	Scandinavian
Ellette	Little elf	French
Elswyth	Elf from the willow trees	English
Elva	Elfin	Old English
Elvia	Elfin	Old English
Elvina	Elfin	Old English
Elwine	Elf wise friend	English
Elwyna	Elf wise friend	English
Engel	Angel	German
Erlene	Noblewoman	English
Erlina	Noblewoman	English
Erline	Noblewoman	English
Esma	Emerald	French
Esme	Emerald	French
Ethal	Noble	Old English
Eugenia	Well born or noble	French
Faline	Catlike	Latin

Fancy	Whimsical	English
Fanny	Free	American
Felice	Fortunate or happy	Latin
Flair	Style or verve	English
Flora	Flower	Latin
Florence	Blooming or flowering	Latin
Frederica	Peaceful ruler	German
Garyn	Mighty with a spear	English
Gay	Light hearted	French
Gayna	White wave	English
Gemma	Precious stone	Latin
Georgina	Farmer	English
Gillian	Downy bearded	Latin
Gladys	Princess	Irish
Glenna	Secluded valley or glen	Irish
Guinevere	White wave	Welsh
Gwen	White wave	Welsh
Gwendolyn	White wave	Welsh
Harriet	Ruler of an enclosure	French
Henrietta	Ruler of the enclosure	English
Hild	Battle maid	German
Hilda	Battle maid	German
Hollis	Near the holly bushes	Old English
Jetta	A deep or glossy black	Greek
Joan	God is gracious	Hebrew
Jody	Praised	American
Juliana	Downy bearded or youthful	Latin
Katie	Pure	English
Keeley	Brave warrior	Irish
Kendra	Knowing	Old english
Leila	Dark beauty	Hebrew
Lilian	Lily	Latin
Linette	Bird	French
Linn	Waterfall	English
Lizbeth	Consecrated to God	English
Lois	Famous warrior	German
Lora	Crowned with laurels	Latin

Loretta	Crowned with laurels	English
Lorna	Crowned with laurels	Latin
Lucetta	Bringer of light	English
Lyn	Waterfall	English
Lynet	Idol	Welsh
Lynette	Idol	Welsh
Lynn	Waterfall	English
Lynna	Waterfall	English
Lynne	Waterfall	English
Mae	Great	English
Maida	Maiden	English
Mariam	Bitter or sea of bitterness	Hebrew
Marian	Bitter or sea of bitterness	English
Maud	Mighty battle maiden	English
Maureen	Bitter	Irish
Maxine	The greatest	Latin
May	To increase	Latin
Mayda	Maiden	Unknown
Megan	Pearl	Irish
Meghan	Pearl	Irish
Mercia	Compassion	English
Meryl	Blackbird	Latin
Mildred	Gentle advisor	Old english
Moira	Sea of bitterness	Irish
Moire	Sea of bitterness	French
Mona	Noble	Irish
Nelda	From the Alder trees	Unknown
Noreen	Bright torch	Greek
Norma	Man from the north	German
Octavia	Eighth	Italian
Odelia	Wealthy	French
Odelina	Wealthy	French
Odelinda	Wealthy	French
Odella	Wealthy	French
Odelyn	Wealthy	French
Odelyna	Wealthy	French
Odette	Wealthy	French

Odilia	Wealthy	French
Ora	Seacoast	English
Orva	Worth gold	French
Ottilie	Little wealthy one	Unknown
Peace	Calm or tranquil	English
Peggy	Pearl	English
Petra	Rock	Latin
Petula	Rock	English
Philippa	Lover of horses	Greek
Philomena	Lover of strength	Greek
Phyllis	Leaf	Greek
Polly	Small	Latin
Portia	Pig	Latin
Primrose	Primrose	English
Prudence	Provident	Latin
Queenie	Queen	Old english
Quenna	Queen	Old English
Randi	Wolf shield	German
Rexanne	Gracious king	English
Rexella	King of light	English
Rowena	White haired	Welsh
Sheena	God is gracious	Hebrew
Shelley	From the ledge meadow	English
Sibley	Fiendly	English
Silver	Lustrous	Old English
Silvia	Of the woods	Latin
Sunn	Cheerful	English
Sunniva	Gift of the sun	Scandinavian
Synne	Cheerful	English
Synnove	Gift of the sun	Unknown
Tait	Pleasant and bright	Old English
Taite	Pleasant and bright	Old English
Tate	Pleasant and bright	Old English
Tayte	Pleasant and bright	English
Thea	Goddess	Greek
Udela	Wealthy	English
Udele	Wealthy	English

Verona	Bringer of victory	Italian
Wanda	Young tree	German
Whitney	White island	Old english
Wilda	Wild	German
Willa	Resolute protector	German
Wilona	Hoped for	English
Wilone	Hoped for	English
Zara	Princess	Hebrew
Zelda	Companion	Old english
BOYS	**MEANING**	**ORIGIN**
Aart	Like an eagle	English
Ace	Unity	Latin
Acey	Unity	Latin
Acton	Town by the oak tree	Old English
Acwel	Kills	Unknown
Acwellen	Kills	Unknown
Aidan	Little fiery one	Irish
Aiken	Oaken	English
Alban	Town on the white hill	Latin
Alden	Old and wise protector	Old English
Aldin	Old and wise protector	Old English
Aldred	Wise counselor	English
Aldwyn	Old friend	English
Alfred	Wise counselor	Old English
Algar	Noble spearman	German
Alger	Noble spearman	German
Almund	Defender of the temple	Unknown
Alton	From the old town	Old English
Alwin	Noble friend	German
Anson	Divine	German
Archard	Sacred	Unknown
Archerd	Sacred	Unknown
Archibald	Bold	German
Arian	Echanted	Greek
Arlice	Honorable	Unknown
Arlys	Honorable	Unknown
Arlyss	Honorable	Unknown

Artair	Bear	Scottish
Arth	Rock	English
Aston	Eastern settlement	English
Audley	Prosperous guardian or old friend	English
Averil	Wild boar	English
Averill	Wild boar	English
Avery	Elf ruler	English
Banning	Small and fair	Irish
Bar	From the birch meadow	English
Barclay	From the birch tree meadow	English
Barney	Son of comfort	English
Barrett	Commerce	French
Barton	From the barley settlement	Old English
Basil	Kingly	Latin
Baxter	Baker	Old English
Bede	Prayer	English
Berkeley	From the birch tree meadow	English
Bernard	Brave as a bear	German
Bertram	Bright raven	English
Betlic	Splendid	English
Boden	Messenger	French
Boniface	To do good	Latin
Bordan	From the boar valley	English
Borden	From the boar valley	English
Brant	Proud	Old English
Brecc	Freckled	Irish
Brice	Strength or valor	Welsh
Brigham	Dwells at the bridge	Old English
Bron	Brown or dark	English
Bronson	Son of the dark man	English
Brun	Dark skinned	German
Bryce	Strength or valor	Welsh
Burgess	Town dweller	English
Burton	From the fortified town	Old English
Byron	At the cowshed	Old English
Camden	From the winding valley	Scottish

Camdene	From the winding valley	Scottish
Cary	Descendant of the dark one	Welsh
Cecil	Dim sighted or blind	Latin
Cerdic	Beloved	Welsh
Chad	Warrior	Old English
Chapman	Merchant	English
Chester	Rocky fortress	Old English
Clifford	Ford near the cliff	Old English
Clive	Cliff by the river	Old English
Colby	Dark or dark haired	Old English
Corey	Dweller near a hollow	Irish
Cosmo	Order or harmony	Greek
Courtland	From the court's land	English
Courtnay	Courtier or court attendant	English
Courtney	Courtier or court attendant	English
Creighton	Dweller by the rocks	English
Cyril	Master or Lord	Greek
Daegal	Dweller by the dark stream	English
Dalston	From Dougal's place	English
Delbert	Bright as day	English
Dell	Hollow or valley	Old English
Deman	Man	Scandinavian
Denby	From the Danish settlement	Scandinavian
Denton	Settlement in the valley	Old English
Derian	Small rocky hill	English
Desmond	From south Munster	Irish
Devon	Poet	Irish
Devyn	Poet	Irish
Dougal	Dark stranger	Scottish
Douglas	Dark stream or dark river	Scottish
Drew	Manly	English
Dudley	The people's meadow	Old English
Duke	Leader	French
Durwin	Friend of the deer	English
Durwyn	Friend of the deer	English
Eamon	Wealthy guardian	Irish
Earl	Nobleman	English

Earle	Nobleman	English
Eddison	Son of Edward	English
Edgar	Lucky spearman	Old English
Edgard	Lucky spearman	Old English
Edlin	Wealthy friend	English
Edlyn	Wealthy friend	English
Edmond	Prosperous protector	Old English
Edmund	Prosperous protector	Old English
Edric	Wealthy ruler	English
Edsel	Rich mans house	English
Edson	Son of Edward	English
Edward	Wealthy guardian	Old English
Edwin	Prosperous friend	Old English
Edwyn	Prosperous friend	Old English
Egbert	Bright sword	English
Eldon	Foreign hill	Old English
Eldred	Old and wise advisor	English
Eldrid	Old and wise advisor	English
Eldwin	Old and wise friend	English
Eldwyn	Old and wise friend	English
Elmer	Noble	Old English
Emmet	Industrious	German
Erian	Enchanted	Greek
Erol	Courageous	Turkish
Errol	Wanderer	Latin
Esmond	Wealthy protector	English
Faran	Baker	Arabic
Felix	Fortunate or happy	Latin
Fenton	Marshland farm	Old English
Feran	Traveler	Old english
Finian	Light skinned	Irish
Firman	Firm or strong	French
Fleming	Dutchman from Flanders	Old English
Fletcher	Arrow maker	Old English
Floyd	Gray or white haired	English
Ford	Dweller near the ford	Old English
Freeman	Free man	English

Gaderian	Gathers	Unknown
Galan	Healer	Greek
Gar	Spear	English
Gareth	Gentle	Welsh
Garr	Spear	English
Garrett	Mighty with a spear	Irish
Garvin	Friend in battle	Old English
Geoff	Peaceful	English
Geoffrey	Peaceful	English
Geraint	Old	English
Gerard	Brave with a spear	Old English
Gervaise	Honorable	French
Giles	Shield bearer	French
Godric	Rules with God	Unknown
Godwine	Friend of God	Old English
Gordie	Hill near the meadow	Old English
Gordon	Hill near the meadow	Old English
Gordy	Hill near the meadow	Old English
Graeme	Grand home	Scottish
Graham	Grand home	English
Grahem	Grand home	English
Gram	Grand home	English
Grimm	Fierce	English
Grimme	Fierce	English
Grindan	Sharp	Unknown
Hall	That which is covered	Old English
Ham	Hot	Hebrew
Holt	Forest	English
Hugh	Bright mind	English
Ingram	Angel	Old English
Irwin	Sea friend	English
Irwyn	Sea friend	English
Ivor	Archer's bow	Scandinavia
Jarvis	Servant with a spear	German
Jeffrey	Divinely peaceful	Old English
Judd	Praised	Hebrew
Kendrick	Royal ruler	Scottish

Kendryek	Son of henry	Irish
Kenric	Royal ruler	English
Kenton	The royal settlement	Old English
Kenway	Brave warrior	Old English
Kim	Warrior chief	Old English
Kimball	Warrior chief	English
King	Monarch	Old English
Kingsley	From the King's meadow	Old English
Kipp	From the pointed hill	Old English
Landry	Ruler	Old English
Lang	Tall man	Scandinavian
Lange	Tall man	Scandinavian
Lar	Crowned with laurels	Scandinavian
Leanian	Lion man or brave as a lion	Greek
Leax	Salmon	Unknown
Leighton	From the meadow farm	Old English
Leland	From the meadow land	Old English
Leng	Tall man	Scandinavian
Lex	Defender of mankind	Greek
Lin	Lives by the linden tree hill	English
Linn	Lives by the linden tree hill	English
Lister	Dyer	English
Lloyd	Grey haired	Welsh
Lucan	Bringer of light	Old English
Lunden	From London	English
Lyn	Waterfall	English
Lyndon	Lives by the linden tree hill	Old English
Lynn	Waterfall	English
Magen	Protector	Hebrew
Mann	Hero	German
Mannix	Monk	Irish
Manton	From the hero's town	English
Maxwell	Dweller by the spring	Scottish
Merlin	Sea hill	Celtic
Merton	Sea town	English
Montgomery	From the wealthy man's mountain	Old English

Morton	Town by thr moor	Old English
Ned	Wealthy guardian	English
Nerian	Protects	Unknown
Neville	New town	French
Newton	From the new town	English
Nodin	Wind	American
Norman	Norseman	French
Norris	Northerner	French
Norton	From the north farm	English
Norvel	From the north town	English
Norville	From the north town	French
Nyle	Island	English
Octe	A son of Hengist	Unknown
Odel	Forested hill	English
Odell	Forested hill	English
Odi	Ruler	Scandinavian
Odin	God of all	Old Norse
Odon	Ruler	Scandinavian
Ody	Ruler	Scandinavian
Orde	Beginning	Latin
Ormod	Bear mountain	English
Orson	Bear like	Latin
Orville	Golden village	French
Orvin	Brave friend or spear friend	English
Orvyn	Brave friend or spear friend	English
Osmond	Divine protection	Old English
Osric	Divine ruler	English
Oswald	Divine power	Old English
Oswin	Divine friend	Old English
Page	Attendent	French
Paige	Attendent	French
Patton	Warrior's town	Old English
Pax	Peaceful	Latin
Paxton	Peaceful town	Latin
Payne	Man from the country	Latin
Pearce	Rock	English
Pearson	Son of Peter	English

Perry	Dweller by the pear tree	English
Pierce	Rock	English
Piers	Lover of horses	English
Putnam	Dweller by the pond	English
Ramm	Ram	English
Rand	Wolf's shield	Old English
Randolf	Wolf shield	Scandinavian
Rawlins	Famous in the land	French
Ray	Dear brook	English
Rice	Noble or rich	English
Ripley	Meadow near the river	English
Ro	Red haired	English
Roan	Tree with red berries	English
Roe	Deer	English
Row	Red haired	English
Rowan	Tree with red berries	English
Rowe	Red haired	English
Roweson	Son of the redhead	English
Rowson	Son of the redhead	English
Ryce	Powerful	English
Seaton	Town near the sea	English
Seaver	Fierce stronghold	English
Selwin	Friend at court	English
Selwyn	Friend at court	English
Sener	Bringer of joy	Turkish
Sever	Fierce stronghold	English
Seward	Sea gaurdian	Old English
Sheldon	Farm on the ledge	Old English
Shelley	From the ledge meadow	Old English
Shelny	From the ledge farm	Old English
Shepard	Shepherd	English
Shephard	Shepherd	English
Sheply	From the sheep meadow	English
Sherard	Of glorious valor	English
Sherwin	Quick as the wind	English
Sherwyn	Quick as the wind	English
Steadman	Dwells at the farm	English

Stedman	Dwells at the farm	English
Stepan	Exalts	Russian
Stewart	Steward	Old English
Stewert	Steward	Old English
Stillman	Quiet	English
Stilwell	From the tranquil stream	English
Storm	Tempestuous	English
Stuart	Steward	Old English
Sutton	Southern town	Old English
Tamar	Palm tree	Hebrew
Tedman	Protector of the land	Old English
Tedmund	Protector of the land	Old English
Teller	Storyteller	Old English
Tolan	From the taxed land	Old English
Toland	From the taxed land	Old English
Torr	Watchtower	Old English
Trace	Harvester	Greek
Tracey	Harvester	Greek
Tracy	Harvester	Greek
Tredan	Tramples	English
Treddian	Leaves	English
Upton	From the high town	Old English
Verge	Staff bearer	Latin
Vernon	Youthful or springlike	Latin
Virgil	Staff bearer	Latin
Wallace	From Wales	English
Wallis	From Wales	English
Ward	Watchman	Old English
Ware	Cautious	Old English
Whitney	From the white island	Old English
Wilbur	Walled stronghold	Old English
Wilfrid	Resolute peacemaker	English
Winchell	Bend in the road	Old English
Winston	Friendly town	Old English
Woodrow	Dweller by the wood	Old English
Wylie	Enchanting	English
Wyman	Fighter	English

Wynchell	Drawer of water	English
Wyne	Friend	English

Biblical

Biblical names never go out of style, no matter where you are in the world – they've been among the most popular names for boys and girls for centuries, and most likely will for many years to come. Many of these names cross reference other sections of the book, especially Anglo Saxon names. Read on for a selection of interesting baby names from the good book, from the standard and well known (John) to the more unusual (Huldah, Meshach).

GIRLS	MEANING	ORIGIN
Abigail	My father rejoices	Hebrew
Abihail	Strong father	Hebrew
Ahinoam	Brother's grace	Hebrew
Anna	Grace	English
Athalia	The Lord is exalted	Hebrew
Azubah	Forsaken	Hebrew
Bathsheba	Daugther of Sheba	Hebrew
Berenice	She will bring victory	Greek
Bilhah	Bashful	Hebrew
Chloe	Blooming	Greek
Claudia	Lame	Latin
Deborah	Bee	Hebrew
Delilah	Delicate	Hebrew
Dinah	Avenged or vindicated	Hebrew
Drusilla	The strong one	Latin
Elisabeth	God is my oath	Hebrew
Esther	Star	Arabic
Eve	Life	Hebrew
Hannah	Gracious	Hebrew
Jael	Mountain goat	Hebrew
Jemimah	Little dove	Hebrew

Joanna	God is gracious	English
Judith	From Judea	Hebrew
Keturah	Incense	Hebrew
Leah	Tired or weary	Hebrew
Lydia	Woman from Lydia	Greek
agdalene	From the high tower	English
Mahalath	Lyre	Arabic
Mara	Bitter sorrow	Hebrew
Martha	Sorrow	Arabic
Mary	Sea of bitterness	Hebrew
Michal	Who is like God	Hebrew
Miriam	Sea of bitterness	Hebrew
Naomi	Beautiful	Hebrew
Orpah	Fawn	Hebrew
Priscilla	Ancient, old or primitive	Latin
Rachel	Innocence of a lamb	Hebrew
Rebecca	Bound	Hebrew
Ruth	Friendship	Hebrew
Salome	Peace	Hebrew
Sarah	Princess	Hebrew
Tabitha	Gazelle	Arabic
Tamar	Palm tree	Hebrew
Zilpah	Dignified	Hebrew
Zipporah	Bird	Hebrew
BOYS	**MEANING**	**ORIGIN**
Aaron	Exalted one	Hebrew
Abel	Breath	Hebrew
Abner	Father of light	Hebrew
Abraham	Father of a multitude	Hebrew
Abram	Exalted father	Hebrew
Adam	Red earth	Hebrew
Amos	Burden	Hebrew
Andrew	Manly	Greek
Asa	Healer	Hebrew
Barak	Lightning	Hebrew
Barnabas	Exalted	Arabic

Bartholmew	Ploughman	Hebrew
Benjamin	Born of the right hand	Hebrew
Cain	Gatherer	Hebrew
Caleb	Faithful dog	Hebrew
Dan	God is my judge	Hebrew
Daniel	God is my judge	Hebrew
David	Beloved	Hebrew
Eleazar	God has helped	Hebrew
Eli	Uplifted or ascent	Hebrew
Elijah	The Lord is my God	Hebrew
Elisha	God is my salvation	Hebrew
Enoch	Consecrated or dedicated	Hebrew
Ephraim	Doubly fruitful	Hebrew
Esau	Hairy	Hebrew
Ezekiel	Strength of God	Hebrew
Gabriel	God is my strength	Hebrew
Gideon	Tree cutter	Hebrew
Hezekiah	God is my strength	Hebrew
Hosea	Salvation	Hebrew
Isaac	Laughter	Hebrew
Isaiah	God is my salvation	Hebrew
Israel	Contender with God	Hebrew
Jacob	Supplanter	Hebrew
James	Supplanter	English
Japheth	He enlarges	Hebrew
Jason	Healer	Greek
Jedidah	Friend of God or beloved of God	Hebrew
Jeremiah	God will uplift	Hebrew
Jesse	Wealthy	Hebrew
Jesus	Jehovah is salvation	Hebrew
Jethro	Overflowing or abundance	Hebrew
Joel	God is willing	Hebrew
John	God is gracious	Hebrew
Jonah	Dove	Hebrew

Jonathan	Gift of God	Hebrew
Joseph	God will add	Hebrew
Joshua	God is salvation	Hebrew
Levi	Joined or united	Hebrew
Luke	Bringer of light	Latin
Malachi	Messenger of God	Hebrew
Mark	Warlike	Latin
Matthew	Gift from God	Hebrew
Matthias	Gift from God	Hebrew
Meshach	Agile	Hebrew
Micah	Who is like God	Hebrew
Michael	Who is like God	Hebrew
Mordecai	Little man	Hebrew
Moses	Drawn out of the water	Hebrew
Nathan	Gift from God	Hebrew
Nathanel	Gift of God	Hebrew
Noah	Rest or comfort	Hebrew
Paul	Small	Latin
Peter	Rock	Latin
Phillip	Lover of horses	Greek
Rueben	Behold a son	Hebrew
Samson	Brght sun	Hebrew
Samuel	Heard by God	Hebrew
Saul	Asked of God	Hebrew
Seth	Appointed	Hebrew
Shem	Renowned	Hebrew
Silas	Asked for	Arabic
Simeon	God is heard	French
Simon	God is heard	Hebrew
Solomon	Peaceful	Hebrew
Stephen	Crown	Greek
Thomas	Twin	Greek
Timothy	One who honors God	Greek
Uriah	God is my light	Hebrew
Zachariah	God remembers	Hebrew
Zebedee	God has given	Hebrew

Zechariah	God remembers	Hebrew
Zedekiah	God is rigtheous	Hebrew
Zephaniah	God has hidden	Hebrew

Chinese

Chinese names come from over 5,000 years of culture and heritage that is impossible to replace. Many of these names symbolize ancient values, virtues, and treasures. There are many different dialects, giving each name its own importance and meaning. Many of the following names come from Buddhism, Taoism, Confucianism, and literary history. Some well-known names in Bai (person of purity) and Kaili (deity).

GIRLS	MEANING	ORIGIN
Ah lam	Like an orchid	Chinese
An	Peace	Chinese
Chu hua	Chrysanthemum	Chinese
Chun	Spring	Chinese
Da xia	Long summer	Chinese
Fang	Fragrant	Chinese
Fang hua	Fragrant flower	Chinese
Hua	Flower	Chinese
Hui fang	Nice flower	Chinese
Jing wei	Small bird	Chinese
Lian	Graceful willow	Chinese
Lien	Lotus	Chinese
Lien hua	Lotus flower	Chinese
Ling	Delicate	Chinese
Mei	Beautiful	Chinese
Mei hua	Beautiful flower	Chinese
Mei lien	Beautiful lotus	Chinese
Mei xing	Beautiful star	Chinese
Mei zhen	Beautiful pearl	Chinese
Xiao xing	Morning star	Chinese
Yin	Silver	Chinese

BOYS	MEANING	ORIGIN
An	Peace	Chinese
Cong	Intelligent	Chinese
Deshi	Virtuous man	Chinese
Gan	Adventure	Chinese
Huang fu	Rich future	Chinese
Jin	Gold	Chinese
Jing	Pure	Chinese
Kong	Void	Chinese
Li	Strength	Chinese
Liang	Excellent	Chinese
Quon	Bright	Chinese
Shen	Spirit	Chinese
Tung	Universal	Chinese
Yu	Universe	Chinese
Zhuang	Strong	Chinese

German

Can you name all of the children in *The Sound of Music?* If so, you already know quite a few German names. For a classic German name, just think of those children in The Sound of Music and pick a name. (Never mind that they're supposed to be Austrian!) German baby names tend to have strong consonants, like Friedrich, Kurt, Louisa, Brigitta, and Gretel.

GIRLS	MEANING	ORIGIN
Ada	Noble and serene	German
Adal	Noble	German
Adalheid	Noble	German
Adalheida	Noble	German
Adali	Noble	German
Adalicia	Noble	French
Adalie	Noble	German

Adaliz	Noble	French
Adalwolfa	Noble she wolf	German
Adela	Noble	German
Adelaide	Noble	German
Adele	Noble	English
Adelheid	Sweet or noble	German
Adelheide	Sweet or noble	German
Adelina	Noble	English
Adelinda	Noble	English
Adeline	Noble	English
Adelisa	Noble	German
Adelita	Noble	German
Adelle	Noble	German
Adelyte	Has good humor	Unknown
Adette	Sweet or noble	English
Adolpha	Noble she wolf	German
Adrian	Dark	Latin
Adriane	Dark	English
Agatha	Good	Greek
Agathe	Honorable or good	Greek
Aili	Noble	German
Ailis	Noble	Irish
Ailse	Noble	German
Alarica	Rules all	Unknown
Alarice	Rules all	Unknown
Alberta	Noble and bright	German
Albertina	Noble	French
Albertine	Noble	French
Albertyne	Noble	French
Alda	Old or wise	German

Aldona	Wise	German
Aleda	Winged	Unknown
Aleida	Noble	German
Alfonsine	Noble	German
Alfreda	Wise counselor	Old English
Alice	Truthful	Greek
Alicia	Truthful	English
Alida	Small and winged	Latin
Alison	Truthful	Old English
Alisz	Truthful	German
Aliz	Truthful	German
Allaryce	Rules all	Unknown
Aloisia	Famous warrior or famous in battle	German
Alonsa	Eager for battle	English
Aloysia	Famous warrior	German
Alphonsine	Noble	German
Alva	Light skinned	Latin
Alvar	Light skinned	Latin
Alvara	Light skinned	Latin
Alvarie	Light skinned	Latin
Alvie	Light skinned	Latin
Alyda	Archaic	Unknown
Alys	Noble	German
Amalasand	Industrious	German
Amalasanda	Industrious	German
Amalda	Eagle or strong	Unknown
Amara	Eternally beautiful	Greek
Angelika	Messenger	German
Annamaria	Bitter grace	English

Annemarie	Bitter grace	English
Anni	Gracious	English
Antonie	Priceless, inestimable or praiseworthy	Latin
Arabella	Beautiful alter	Latin
Ararinda	Tenacious	Unknown
Arleigh	Meadow of the hare	Old English
Armina	Warrior maiden	German
Baldhart	Bold or strong	German
Ballard	Bold or strong	Unknown
Bathild	Heroine	German
Bathilda	Heroine	German
Bathilde	Heroine	German
Bemadette	Courage of a bear	Unknown
Berdina	Glorious	German
Berdine	Glorious and famous maiden	German
Berit	Glorious	German
Berta	Bright ruler	German
Bertha	Bright ruler	German
Bertina	Bright or shining	English
Binga	From the kettle shaped hollow	Unknown
Binge	From the kettle shaped hollow	Unknown

Blas	Firebrand	German
Blasa	Firebrand	German
Bruna	Dark warrior	German
Brune	Dark warrior	German
Brunhild	Dark warrior	German
Brunhilda	Dark warrior	German
Brunhilde	Dark warrior	German
Cheryl	Beloved	French
Chriselda	Strong	Unknown
Clarimond	Brilliant protectress	Unknown
Clarimonda	Brilliant protectress	Unknown
Clarimonde	Brilliant protectress	Unknown
Claudelle	Lame	French
Claudette	Lame	French
Claudia	Lame	Latin
Claudine	Lame	French
Clotilda	Heroine	German
Clotilde	Heroine	German
Conradina	Bold	German
Conradine	Bold	German
Dagmar	Splendid or glorious day	German
Dagomar	Splendid or glorious day	German
Dell	Bright	German
Della	Bright	German
Delma	Noble protector	Unknown
Delmi	Noble protector	Unknown
Delmira	Noble protector	Unknown
Delmy	Noble protector	Unknown
Didrika	Ruler of the	German

	people	
Eadaion	Joyous friendship	Unknown
Eartha	Earthy	English
Ebba	Strong as a boar	German
Edda	Pleasant	German
Edelina	Gracious or kind	English
Edeline	Gracious or kind	English
Ediline	Gracious or kind	English
Elfrida	Peaceful ruler	German
Elica	God is my oath	Hebrew
Elke	Noble	German
Elma	God's protection	German
Elsa	Noble	German
Else	Noble	German
Elsha	Noble	German
Elsie	Noble	German
Elsje	Noble	German
Elyse	Noble	German
Ema	Industrious	German
Emestina	Industrious	Unknown
Emestine	Industrious	Unknown
Emma	Industrious	German
Emmaline	Industrious	French
Emmalyn	Industrious	American
Emmeline	Industrious	French
Emmy	Industrious	German
Engelbertha	Bright angel	German
Engelbertina	Bright angel	German
Engelbertine	Bright angel	German
Engleberta	Bright angel	German

Eraman	Honorable	Unknown
Eramana	Honorable	Unknown
Erma	Warrior	German
Erna	Sincere	English
Ernesha	Sincere	English
Ernestina	Sincere	English
Ernestine	Sincere	English
Ertha	Earthy	English
Ethel	Noble	Old English
Ethelinda	Noble serpent	English
Ethelinde	Noble serpent	English
Etta	Little one	German
Evon	Archer	French
Evonna	Archer	French
Evonne	Archer	French
Evony	Archer	French
Felda	From the field	Unknown
Felisberta	Intelligent	Unknown
Fernanda	Adventurous	German
Franziska	Free or from France	German
Freda	Peaceful ruler	German
Fredda	Peaceful ruler	German
Freddi	Peaceful ruler	German
Frederica	Peaceful ruler	German
Frederika	Peaceful ruler	German
Fredrika	Peaceful ruler	German
Frieda	Peaceful ruler	German

Name	Meaning	Origin
Fritzi	Peaceful ruler	German
Gabriele	God is my strength	French
Gaelle	My father rejoices	Hebrew
Galiana	Light	Russian
Galiena	Light	Russian
Geneva	Juniper	French
Geneve	Juniper	French
Genevie	White wave	French
Genevieve	White wave	French
Genivee	White wave	French
Genoveva	White wave	German
Genowefa	White wave	German
Georgia	Farmer	Greek
Geraldina	Mighty with a spear	German
Geraldine	Mighty with a spear	French
Geralyn	Rules by the spear	American
Geralynn	Rules by the spear	American
Gerda	Beloved warrior	German
Gerde	Beloved warrior	German
Gerdie	Beloved warrior	German
Gerhardina	Brave with a spear	German
Gerhardine	Brave with a spear	German
Gertrud	Beloved warrior	German
Gertruda	Beloved warrior	German
Gertrude	Beloved	German

	warrior	
Gertrut	Beloved warrior	German
Gerwalt	Mighty with a spear	German
Gerwalta	Mighty with a spear	German
Ghislaine	Oath or pledge	German
Gilberta	Illustrious pledge	German
Gisela	Pledge	Italian/Spanish
Gisella	Pledge	Italian/Spanish
Giselle	Pledge	German
Gisilberhta	Hostage	German
Greta	Pearl	German
Gretchen	Pearl	German
Gretel	Pearl	German
Gricelda	Gray or gray haired	German
Griselda	Gray battle maiden	German
Griselde	Gray battle maiden	German
Grisella	Gray battle maiden	German
Grisjahilde	Gray battle maiden	German
Griswalda	From the gray forest	German
Griswalde	From the gray forest	German
Gryselda	Gray battle maiden	German
Gudrun	Friend in war	Old Norse
Gudruna	Friend in war	Old Norse
Guida	Guide	Unknown
Guilaine	Sweet pledge	French

Gunilla	Battle maiden	German
Gunnel	Battle maiden	German
Gustel	Majestic	Latin
Hadu	Battle maiden	Unknown
Haduwig	Strife	German
Halag	Pious	Unknown
Halfrid	Peaceful heroine	German
Halfrida	Peaceful heroine	German
Halifrid	Peaceful heroine	German
Harimanna	Warrior maiden	German
Harimanne	Warrior maiden	German
Hedda	Battle maiden	German
Hedwig	Battle maiden	German
Hedy	Battle maiden	German
Heida	Noble and serene	German
Heide	Noble and serene	German
Heidi	Noble and serene	German
Helene	Light	French
Helga	Holy or pious	German
Helma	Resolute protector	German
Herta	Child of the earth	Old English
Hertha	Child of the earth	Old English

Name	Meaning	Origin
Hida	Warrior	German
Hide	Warrior	German
Hild	Noble maid	German
Hilda	Battle maid	German
Hildagarde	Fortress	German
Hilde	Battle maid	German
Hildegard	Fortress	German
Hildemar	Glorious	German
Hildemara	Glorious	German
Hildimar	Glorious	German
Hildireth	Battle counselor	German
Hildreth	Battle counselor	German
Hilma	Resolute protector	German
Holda	Hidden	German
Holde	Hidden	German
Holle	Beloved	Unknown
Huberta	Bright mind	German
Hugiherahta	Intelligent	German
Hulda	Enduring or loving	Swedish
Hulde	Beloved	German
Hylda	Battle maid	German
Ida	Hardworking	German
Idaia	Hardworking	German
Idalie	Hardworking	German
Idetta	Hardworking	German
Idette	Hardworking	German
Idna	Hardworking	German
Ilsa	God is my oath	German
Ilse	God is my oath	German
Ilyse	Noble	German
Irma	Warrior	German
Irmgard	War goddess	German

Irmigard	War goddess	German
Irmina	War goddess	German
Irmine	War goddess	German
Irmuska	War goddess	German
Isa	Strong willed	Unknown
Isana	Strong willed	Unknown
Isane	Strong willed	Unknown
Isold	Fair Lady	Welsh
Isolda	Fair lady	Welsh
Isole	Fair lady	Welsh
Jakoba	Supplanter	Hebrew
Jakobe	Supplanter	Hebrew
Jakobie	Supplanter	Hebrew
Johanna	God is gracious	German
Johannah	God is gracious	German
Jolan	Violet flower	Greek
Jolanka	Violet flower	Greek
Joli	Pretty	French
Josefa	God will add	Spanish
Karla	Farmer	German
Karlee	Tiny and feminine	Latin
Karleen	Tiny and feminine	German
Karleigh	Tiny and feminine	German
Karlen	Tiny and feminine	German
Karlene	Tiny and feminine	German
Karlesha	Tiny and feminine	German
Karley	Tiny and feminine	Latin
Karli	Tiny and feminine	Latin

Karlie	Tiny and feminine	Latin
Karlin	Tiny and feminine	German
Karlina	Tiny and feminine	German
Karline	Tiny and feminine	German
Karly	Tiny and feminine	Latin
Karlyn	Tiny and feminine	German
Karola	Tiny and feminine	Slavic
Karolina	Tiny and feminine	Slavic
Karoline	Tiny and feminine	German
Katchen	Pure	German
Katharina	Pure	German
Kathe	Pure	German
Katrina	Pure	German
Kikka	Mistress of all	Unknown
Kuonrada	Wise	Unknown
Landra	Counselor	German
Leoda	Of the people	Unknown
Leonore	Light	Greek
Leopolda	Brave people	German
Leopoldina	Brave people	German
Leopoldine	Brave people	German
Leota	Of the people	German
Liezel	Consecrated to God	German
Lilli	Lily	Latin
Lind	Tender beauty	Spanish

Linda	Tender beauty	Spanish
Lindie	Tender beauty	Spanish
Lisa	Consecrated to God	Hebrew
Lise	Consecrated to God	German
Lisette	Consecrated to God	French
Lorah	Crowned with laurels	Latin
Loraine	From Lorraine	French
Loralei	Alluring	German
Loranna	Crowned with laurels	Latin
Lorelei	Alluring	German
Lorita	Crowned with laurels	Spanish
Lorraine	From Lorraine	French
Lotte	Tiny and feminine	German
Louisane	Famous warrior	German
Louise	Famous warrior	German
Lovisa	Famous warrior	German
Loyce	Famous warrior	German
Luana	Graceful battle maiden	German
Luane	Graceful battle maiden	German
Lucina	Bringer of	Basque

	light	
Ludkhannah	Graceful battle maiden	German
Luete	Of the people	Unknown
Luijzika	Famous warrior	Unknown
Luise	Famous warrior	German
Lujza	Famous warrior	Unknown
Lurleen	Temptress	German
Lurlene	Temptress	German
Lurlina	Temptress	German
Lurline	Temptress	German
Maddalen	From the high tower	Greek
Maddalena	From the high tower	Italian
Maddalene	From the high tower	Greek
Maddalyn	From the high tower	Greek
Madelhari	Army or war counselor	German
Mady	Maiden	German
Maganhildi	Strong battle maiden	German
Magd	From the high tower	German
Magda	From the high tower	Slavic
Magnhilda	Strong battle maiden	German
Magnild	Strong battle maiden	German
Magnilda	Strong battle maiden	German

Magnilde	Strong battle maiden	German
Malene	From the high tower	Scandinavian
Mallory	Unfortunate or unlucky	French
Marelda	Famous battle maiden	German
Margit	Pearl	Hungarian
Margo	Pearl	French
Margrit	Pearl	German
Marhilda	Famous battle maiden	German
Marhildi	Famous battle maiden	German
Maria	Bitter or sea of bitterness	Hebrew
Marilda	Famous battle maiden	German
Maritza	Of the sea	German
Marlaina	From the high tower	Greek
Marlana	From the high tower	English
Marlayna	From the high tower	German
Marlayne	From the high tower	Greek
Marleen	From the high tower	Greek
Marleena	From the high tower	German
Marleene	From the high tower	Greek
Marleina	From the	Greek

	high tower	
Marlena	From the high tower	German
Marlene	From the high tower	Greek
Marlina	From the high tower	German
Marlinda	From the high tower	German
Marline	From the high tower	Greek
Marlis	Bitter	English
Marlisa	Bitter	English
Mathild	Mighty battle maiden	German
Mathilda	Mighty battle maiden	German
Mathilde	Mighty battle maiden	German
Matilda	Mighty battle maiden	German
Melisande	Honey bee	French
Millicent	Industrious	English
Millie	Industrious	English
Mina	Love	German
Mindy	Honey	Greek
Minna	Resolute protector	German
Minne	Resolute protector	German
Mitzi	Sea of bitterness	German
Monika	Solitary	Greek
Nadetta	Hope	French
Nadette	Hope	French

Nadina	Hopeful	Russian
Nadine	Hopeful	Russian
Nadja	Hope	Russian
Nixie	Little water sprite	German
Norberaht	Bright heroine	German
Norberta	Bright heroine	German
Norberte	Bright heroine	German
Nordica	From the north	Unknown
Nordika	From the north	Unknown
Oda	Wealthy	French
Odelina	Wealthy	French
Odette	Wealthy	French
Odiana	Wealthy	French
Odiane	Wealthy	French
Odila	Wealthy	French
Odile	Wealthy	French
Olinda	Defender of the land	Spanish
Ordalf	Elfin spear	Unknown
Ordella	Elfin spear	Unknown
Otilie	Fortunate heroine	Slavic
Otka	Fortunate heroine	Slavic
Otthild	Fortunate heroine	German
Otthilda	Fortunate heroine	German
Otthilde	Fortunate heroine	German
Ottila	Fortunate heroine	German
Ottilia	Fortunate	German

	heroine	
Otylia	Fortunate heroine	German
Perahta	Glorious	Hebrew
Petronilla	Rock	Latin
Petronille	Small rock	Greek
Philipinna	Loves horses	Spanish
Philippine	Loves horses	Spanish
Rachel	Innocence of a lamb	Hebrew
Ricarda	Rich and powerful ruler	Spanish
Rilla	Small brook	German
Rille	Small brook	German
Rillia	Small brook	German
Rillie	Small brook	German
Roch	Glory	German
Roderica	Famous ruler	German
Roderika	Famous ruler	German
Rolanda	Famous in the land	German
Rolande	Famous in the land	German
Romhild	Glorious battle maiden	German
Romhilda	Glorious battle maiden	German
Romhilde	Glorious battle maiden	German
Romilda	Glorious battle maiden	German
Romilde	Glorious battle maiden	German

Rosa	Famous guardian	German
Rosamund	Famous guardian	German
Rosemonde	Famous guardian	German
Rosemunda	Famous guardian	German
Rozmonda	Famous guardian	German
Rozomund	Famous guardian	German
Rudella	Famous wolf	German
Rudelle	Famous wolf	German
Ruomhildi	Glorious battle maiden	German
Rupetta	Famous	German
Rupette	Famous	German
Sarohildi	Armored battle maiden	Unknown
Senta	Assistant	Unknown
Sente	Assistant	Unknown
Serhild	Armored battle maiden	German
Serhilda	Armored battle maiden	German
Serihilda	Armored battle maiden	German
Serihilde	Armored battle maiden	German
Serilda	Armored battle maiden	German

Sigfreda	Victorious peace	German
Sigfrieda	Victorious peace	German
Sigfriede	Victorious peace	German
Sigilwig	Champion	German
Solvig	Champion	Unknown
Suzanne	Lily	English
Tibelda	Boldest	Unknown
Tibelde	Boldest	Unknown
Tibeldie	Boldest	Unknown
Tresa	Harvester	Greek
Truda	Beloved warrior	German
Trudchen	Beloved warrior	German
Trude	Beloved warrior	German
Tugenda	Virtue	Unknown
Uli	Wealthy	Scandinavian
Ulka	Wealthy	Scandinavian
Ulla	Little bear	Latin
Ulrica	Ruler of all	German
Ulrike	World ruler	German
Valborga	Protecting ruler	Unknown
Vanda	Wanderer	German
Vande	Wanderer	German
Verena	Truthful	Latin
Verene	Truthful	Latin
Verina	Truthful	Latin
Viheke	Little woman	Unknown
Viveka	Little woman	Unknown
Walborgd	Protecting ruler	German
Walda	Powerful	German
Waldhurga	Protecting	Unknown

ruler

Name	Meaning	Origin
Wanda	Wanderer	German
Wande	Wanderer	German
Wandy	Wanderer	German
Warda	Guardian	German
Welda	Ruler	German
Wido	Warrior maiden	Unknown
Wilda	Untamed	German
Wilde	Untamed	German
Wilhelmina	Resolute protector	German
Wilhelmine	Resolute protector	German
Wilma	Resolute protector	German
Winifred	Peaceful friend	German
Winifreda	Peaceful friend	German
Winifrid	Peaceful friend	German
Winifride	Peaceful friend	German
Winola	Gracious friend	German
Yseult	Ice ruler	German

BOYS	MEANING	ORIGIN
Abelard	Resolute	German
Adal	Noble	German
Adalard	Brave	German
Adalbert	Intelligent or noble	German
Adalgar	Noble spearman	German
Adalhard	Brave	German
Adalric	Noble friend	German
Adalrik	Noble friend	German

Adalwen	Noble friend	German
Adalwin	Noble friend	German
Adalwine	Noble friend	German
Adalwolf	Noble wolf	German
Adel	Brave	German
Adelbert	Noble	German
Adelhard	Resolute	German
Adlar	Eagle	German
Adler	Eagle	German
Adne	Nobleman's island	English
Adolf	Noble wolf	German
Adolfo	Noble wolf	German
Adolph	Noble wolf	German
Adolphus	Noble wolf	German
Agustine	Majestic	Latin
Ahren	Eagle	Unknown
Ailbe	Intelligent or noble	Unknown
Aksel	Father of peace	Danish
Alaric	Noble leader	German
Alarick	Noble leader	German
Alarik	Noble leader	German
Albert	Noble and bright	German
Albrecht	Intelligent or noble	German
Ald	Old or wise	Italian
Aldo	Old or wise	Italian
Aldrik	Old or wise counselor	English
Alfonso	Noble and eager	Italian
Alger	Noble spearman	German
Alhmanic	Divine	German
Alhsom	Sacred fame	Unknown

Alhwin	Noble friend	Unknown
Alois	Famous warrior or famous in battle	German
Alphonso	Ready	Italian
Alric	Rules all	German
Alrick	Rules all	German
Alrik	Noble leader	German
Altman	Wise man	German
Altmann	Wise man	German
Alvar	Army of elves	English
Alvaro	Elf army	Spanish
Alvin	Noble friend	German
Alvy	Noble friend	German
Alwin	Noble friend	German
Amald	Power of an eagle	German
Amall	Power of an eagle	German
Amaud	Power of an eagle	German
Amd	Power of an eagle	German
Amdt	Power of an eagle	German
Ame	Eagle	Unknown
Amell	Power of an eagle	Unknown
Amery	Industrious leader	German
Amet	Power of an eagle	German
Amett	Power of an eagle	German
Amey	Eagle	German
Amhold	Power of an eagle	German

Ami	Eagle	German
Amo	Power of an eagle	German
Amold	Power of an eagle	German
Amoll	Power of an eagle	German
Amory	Industrious leader	German
Amot	Power of an eagle	German
Amott	Power of an eagle	German
Amwolf	Eagle wolf	German
Andreas	Manly	Greek
Ann	Gift of God	German
Ansel	God's protection	French
Ansell	God's protection	French
Anselmo	Divine protection	Spanish
Ansgar	From Germanic elements ans - god & gar - spear	German
Anson	Divine	German
Anton	Priceless, inestimable or praiseworthy	German
Apsel	Father of peace	German
Archard	Strong	Unknown
Archibald	Bold	German
Archimbald	Bold	German
Ardal	Eagle ruler	German
Are	Eagle	Danish

Aren	Eagle	Danish
Arend	Power of an eagle	Danish
Aric	Noble leader	German
Arick	Noble leader	German
Arik	Noble leader	German
Armand	Soldier	German
Armando	Soldier	Spanish
Arnold	Eagle ruler	German
Arnt	Eagle ruler	German
Arvin	Friend of the people	German
Audric	Old or wise ruler	English
Audrick	Old or wise ruler	English
Audwin	Wise ruler	English
Audwine	Wise ruler	English
Augustine	Majestic	Latin
Augustus	Majestic	Latin
Aurick	Noble leader	German
Aurik	Noble leader	German
Axel	Source of life	German
Baldemar	Princely	German
Baldric	Bold	German
Baldrik	Bold	German
Balduin	Bold friend	German
Baldwin	Bold friend	German
Baldwyn	Bold friend	German
Baltasar	Protected by God	Arabic
Bamard	Brave as a bear	German
Bamey	Brave as a bear	German
Bannan	Commander	Unknown
Bannruod	Famous commander	German

Barnard	Strong as a bear	French
Barret	Mighty as a bear	German
Barrett	Brave as a bear	German
Bartram	Illustrious	German
Bem	Bear	German
Bemelle	Strong as a bear	French
Bemot	Brave as a bear	French
Benat	Brave as a bear	Unknown
Ber	Bear	Unknown
Berchtwald	Bright ruler	German
Berdy	Intelligent	English
Berend	Brave as a bear	German
Berg	Mountain	German
Berinhard	Brave as a bear	German
Berlyn	Son of Berl	German
Bernard	Brave as a bear	German
Bernardo	Brave as a bear	Spanish
Bernardyn	Brave as a bear	German
Bernd	Brave as a bear	German
Berne	Brave as a bear	German
Bernhard	Brave as a bear	German
Bernon	Brave as a bear	German
Berowalt	Mighty as a bear	German

Berrin	Bear	German
Berthold	Bright ruler	German
Bertram	Illustrious	German
Bing	From the kettle shaped hollow	Unknown
Binge	From the kettle shaped hollow	Unknown
Bittan	Desire	Unknown
Bitten	Desire	Unknown
Boell	Hill dweller	Unknown
Bogart	Bowstring	German
Bogohardt	Bowstring	German
Brand	Fiery torch	Unknown
Brandeis	Dwells on a burned clearing	Unknown
Bren	Little raven	Irish
Brendan	Little raven	Irish
Brendis	Little raven	Irish
Brock	Stream	German
Bronson	Brown's son	German
Bruno	Brown	German
Brunon	Brown	German
Burhardt	Strong as a castle	German
Burkhart	Strong as a castle	German
Burlin	Son of Berl	German
Burnard	Strong or brave as a bear	German
Burnell	Strong or brave as a bear	German

68

Carl	Farmer	German
Charles	Manly	English
Chlodwig	Famous warrior	German
Christofer	Christ bearer	Greek
Christoffer	Christ bearer	Greek
Clovis	Renowned warrior	German
Conrad	Honest or brave advisor	German
Conradin	Honest or brave advisor	German
Conrado	Honest or brave advisor	Spanish
Cord	Honest advisor	German
Corrado	Bold or wise counsel	Spanish
Cort	Honest advisor	German
Dagoberto	Splendid or glorious day	Spanish
Darek	Ruler of the people	German
Dearg	Red haired	German
Dedric	Ruler of the people	German
Dedrick	Ruler of the people	German
Dedrik	Ruler of the people	German
Dereck	Ruler of the people	German
Derek	Ruler of the people	German
Derick	Ruler of the	German

	people	
Derik	Ruler of the people	German
Derrek	Ruler of the people	German
Derrick	Ruler of the people	German
Derrik	Ruler of the people	German
Derry	Red haired	Irish
Deryck	Ruler of the people	German
Deryk	Ruler of the people	German
Deutsch	A German	German
Dick	Rich and powerful ruler	German
Diederich	Ruler of the people	German
Diedrick	Ruler of the people	German
Dierck	Ruler of the people	German
Dieter	Ruler of the people	German
Dietrich	Ruler of the people	German
Dietz	Ruler of the people	German
Dirk	Ruler of the people	Scandinavian
Dolphus	Noble wolf	German
Drud	Strong	German
Drugi	Strong	German
Dutch	From Germany	German
Earnest	Sincere	English
Eberhard	Strong as a	German

	boar	
Eberhardt	Strong as a boar	German
Eburhardt	Strong as a boar	German
Eckerd	Sacred	German
Edel	Noble	German
Edingu	Famous ruler	Unknown
Edlin	Wealthy friend	English
Edsel	Noble or bright	German
Eduard	Wealthy guardian	German
Edward	Wealthy guardian	Old English
Edwin	Prosperous friend	Old English
Edwyn	Prosperous friend	Old English
Eginhard	Strong with a sword	German
Eginhardt	Strong with a sword	German
Egon	Strong with a sword	German
Ehren	Honorable	German
Einhard	Strong with a sword	German
Einhardt	Strong with a sword	German
Ekerd	Sacred	German
Ekhard	Sacred	German
Elbert	Bright or famous	German
Ellery	From the elder tree island	English
Eloy	Chosen one	Latin

Ely	Uplifted or ascent	Hebrew
Emerson	Industrious ruler	German
Emery	Industrious ruler	German
Emest	Serious	German
Emil	Industrious	German
Emo	Serious	Unknown
Emory	Industrious ruler	German
Emst	Serious	Unknown
Enando	Bold venture	Unknown
Engel	Angel	German
Englbehrt	Bright angel	German
Englebert	Bright angel	German
Enno	Strong with a sword	Unknown
Eno	Strong with a sword	Unknown
Erchanbold	Sacred or bold	German
Erchanhardt	Sacred or bold	German
Erhard	Honor	German
Erhardt	Honor	German
Erich	Eternal ruler	Scandinavian
Erkerd	Sacred	German
Ernest	Sincere	English
Errol	Wanderer	Latin
Erroll	Wanderer	Latin
Eugen	Well born or noble	German
Everard	Strong as a wild boar	German
Evert	Strong as a boar	Dutch
Evrard	Strong as a	German

	boar	
Eward	Strong as a boar	German
Ewart	Strong as a boar	German
Falk	Falconer	Latin
Falke	Falconer	Latin
Falken	Falconer	Latin
Fonsie	Noble and eager	German
Fonso	Noble and eager	German
Fonzell	Noble and eager	German
Fonzie	Noble and eager	German
Fonzo	Noble and eager	German
Frantz	Free or from France	German
Franz	Free or from France	German
Fred	Peaceful ruler	German
Freddie	Peaceful ruler	German
Freddy	Peaceful ruler	German
Frederick	Peaceful ruler	German
Fremont	Noble protector	German
Friedrich	Peaceful ruler	German
Friedrick	Peaceful ruler	German
Frimunt	Noble protector	German
Fritz	Peaceful	German

	ruler	
Garan	Guards or guardian	English
Garen	Mighty with a spear	English
Garey	Mighty with a spear	Old English
Garin	Mighty with a spear	English
Garion	Mighty with a spear	English
Garon	Mighty with a spear	English
Garren	Mighty with a spear	English
Garrey	Mighty with a spear	English
Garrick	Spear ruler	Old English
Garrin	Mighty with a spear	English
Garrison	Spear fortified town	English
Garron	Mighty with a spear	English
Garry	Mighty with a spear	English
Garson	Spear fortified town	Old English
Garvyn	Friend in battle	Old English
Gary	Mighty with a spear	English
Geomar	Famous in battle	Unknown
Georg	Farmer	Dutch
Gerald	Mighty with a spear	German

74

Name	Meaning	Origin
Gerard	Brave with a spear	Old English
Gere	Rules with a spear	German
Gerhard	Brave with a spear	German
Gerlach	Spear thrower	Dutch
Gerold	Mighty with a spear	Danish
Geron	Mighty with a spear	English
Gerrald	Mighty with a spear	German
Gerrard	Brave with a spear	English
Gerrell	Mighty with a spear	English
Ghislain	Oath or pledge	German
Gilbert	Illustrious pledge	English
Gilleasbuig	Bold	Unknown
Giomar	Famous in battle	Unknown
Goddard	Divinely firm	German
Godfrey	God's peace	German
Gofried	God's peace	German
Gottfried	God's peace	German
Gregor	Vigilant watchman	Greek
Gretel	Pearl	German
Griswald	From the gray forest	German
Griswold	From the gray forest	German
Gunther	Battler warrior	Scandinavian
Gustav	Staff of the	Old Norse

	Goths	
	Staff of the	
Gustave	Goths	Scandinavian
	Little	
Hacket	woodcutter	German
	Little	
Hackett	woodcutter	German
	From the	
Hamlet	little villiage	French
	From the	
Hamlett	little villiage	French
	Ruler of the	
Hamlin	estate	German
	From the	
Hamoelet	little home	Unknown
	God is	
Han	gracious	Scandinavian
	God is	
Hann	gracious	Scandinavian
	God is	
Hanno	gracious	German
	God is	
Hans	gracious	Scandinavian
	God is	
Hanz	gracious	Scandinavian
Hardtman	Strong	German
Hardy	Daring	German
Hariman	Protective	German
Harimann	Protective	German
Harti	Daring	Unknown
Hartman	Strong	German
Hartmann	Strong	German
	Army	
Harvey	warrior	German
	Ruler of an	
Heinrich	enclosure	German
Helmut	Brave	German
Helmutt	Brave	German
Henry	Ruler of the	German

	enclosure	
Herbert	Illustrious warrior	German
Herman	Soldier	German
Hernando	Adventurous	Spanish
Herrick	Army leader	German
Hewett	Little smart one	German
Hewitt	Little smart one	German
Hewlett	Little smart one	German
Hewlitt	Little smart one	German
Hildbrand	War sword	German
Hildehrand	War sword	German
Hobard	Bert's hill	German
Hobart	Bert's hill	German
Hobbard	Bert's hill	German
Hoh	High	German
Hohberht	Bert's hill	German
How	High	German
Howe	High	German
Hubbard	Bright mind	German
Hubert	Bright mind	German
Hugo	Bright mind	Latin
Hulbard	Graceful	German
Hulbart	Graceful	German
Hulbert	Graceful	German
Huldiberaht	Graceful	German
Humberto	Brilliant strength	Portuguese
Humphrey	Peaceful strength	German
Hunfrid	Peaceful strength	German
Hunfried	Peaceful strength	German

Immanuel	God is with us	Hebrew
Ingall	Angel	German
Ingalls	Angel	German
Ingel	Angel	German
Ingelbert	Bright as an angel	German
Inglebert	Bright as an angel	German
Izaak	Laughter	Hebrew
Jaecar	Hunter	Unknown
Jakob	Supplanter	German
Jansen	God is gracious	Scandinavian
Jantis	Sharp spear	Unknown
Jarman	A German	German
Jarmann	A German	German
Jay	Blue jay	French
Jaye	Blue jay	French
Johan	God is gracious	German
Johann	God is gracious	German
Johannes	God is gracious	German
Josef	God will add	German
Jurgen	Farmer	German
Kaiser	Long haired	German
Karl	Farmer	German
Keefer	Barrel maker	German
Keifer	Barrel maker	German
Kelby	Farm by the spring	German
Kiefer	Barrel maker	German
Klaus	Victorious people	German
Koby	Supplanter	Polish

Koen	Wise counsel or honest advisor	German
Koenraad	Wise counsel or honest advisor	Dutch
Kolby	Dark skinned	Old English
Kolt	Coal town	English
Kolten	Coal town	English
Koltin	Coal town	English
Kolton	Coal town	English
Konni	Wise counsel or honest advisor	German
Konrad	Wise counsel or honest advisor	German
Kord	Wise counsel or honest advisor	German
Kort	Bold	German
Kuhlbert	Calm or bright	German
Kulbart	Calm or bright	German
Kulbert	Calm or bright	German
Kuno	Honest advisor	German
Kunz	Honest advisor	German
Kurt	Wise counsel	German
Kurtis	Courteous	French
Lamar	Famous land	German
Lamarr	Famous land	German
Lambart	Light of land	German
Lambert	Light of land	German
Lambrecht	Light of land	German

Lambret	Light of land	German
Lambrett	Light of land	German
Landmari	Famous land	Unknown
Larenzo	Crowned with laurels	Italian
Laurenz	Crowned with laurels	Latin
Lenard	Brave as a lion	German
Lennard	Brave as a lion	German
Leon	Brave as a lion	German
Leonard	Brave as a lion	German
Leopold	Brave people	German
Leopoldo	Brave people	German
Lewy	Famous or renowned fighter	English
Lindberg	From the linden tree mountain	German
Lindeberg	From the linden tree mountain	German
Lorah	Crowned with laurels	Latin
Lorenz	Crowned with laurels	Spanish
Loring	Son of the famous warrior	German
Loritz	Crowned with laurels	Latin
Lothair	Famous warrior	German
Lothar	Famous warrior	German

Lotharing	Famous warrior	German
Louis	Famous warrior	German
Luduvico	Famous warrior	Italian
Ludwig	Famous warrior	German
Ludwik	Famous warrior	German
Lughaidh	Famous warrior	Unknown
Luigi	Famous warrior	Italian
Luiginw	Famous warrior	Unknown
Luis	Famous warrior	Spanish
Luki	Famous warrior	Basque
Luther	Famous warrior	German
Lutz	Famous warrior	German
Madelhari	Army or war counselor	German
Mallory	Army counselor	German
Mandel	Almond	German
Manfred	Man of peace or peaceful	English
Manfried	Man of peace or peaceful	English
Manfrit	Man of peace or peaceful	German
Margit	Pearl	Hungarian

Markel	Warlike	Latin
Markell	Warlike	Latin
Markos	Warlike	Latin
Markus	Warlike	Latin
Martel	Hammerer	English
Martell	Hammerer	English
Marx	God of war	German
Maximilian	The greatest	Latin
Maximillian	The greatest	Latin
Mayer	Great	Latin
Maynard	Powerful	English
Mayne	Powerful	English
Maynor	Powerful	English
Meinhard	Firm	German
Meinke	Firm	German
Meino	Firm	German
Meinrad	Strong advisor	German
Meinyard	Firm	German
Nardo	Strong or hardy	German
Nef	Nephew	Unknown
Nefen	Nephew	Unknown
Neff	Nephew	Unknown
Nefin	Nephew	Unknown
Nickolaus	Victory of the people	German
Nikolaus	Victorious people	Greek
Norbert	Brilliant hero	Scandinavian
Norberto	Brilliant hero	Scandinavian
Norman	Man of the north	French
Normand	Man of the north	French
Odbart	Wealthy	German
Odhert	Wealthy	German
Orbart	Wealthy	German

Orbert	Wealthy	German
Orlan	Renowned in the land	German
Orland	Renowned in the land	German
Orlando	Renowned in the land	German
Orlin	Renowned in the land	German
Orlondo	Renowned in the land	Spanish
Oswald	Power of God	Old English
Othman	Wealthy	German
Othmann	Wealthy	German
Otho	Wealthy	German
Othomann	Wealthy	German
Otis	Wealthy	German
Otto	Wealthy or prosperious	German
Ottokar	Happy warrior	German
Peer	Rock	English
Penn	Famous commander	German
Penrod	Famous commander	German
Pepin	Petitioner	German
Peppi	Petitioner	German
Per	Rock	Swedish
Raimond	Wise protector	German
Raimundo	Wise protector	Spanish
Rainart	Strong judgment	German
Rainer	Strong counselor	German
Rainhard	Strong	German

	judgment	
Rainor	Strong counselor	German
Rald	Famous leader	German
Rambert	Mighty or intelligent	German
Ramhart	Mighty or intelligent	German
Ramond	Guards wisely	English
Raymond	Wise protector	English
Raymund	Wise protector	English
Raymundo	Wise protector	Spanish
Raynard	Strong councelor	French
Reggie	Powerful ruler	English
Reginald	Powerful ruler	English
Reginhard	Mighty and brave	German
Reginheraht	Mighty or intelligent	German
Reiner	Counsel	German
Reinhard	Bold or courageous	German
Renard	Bold or courageous	French
Renke	Strong judgment	German
Reymond	Guards wisely	German
Reymundo	Guards wisely	Spanish
Reynald	King's	English

	advisor	
Reynard	Bold or courageous	French
Reynold	King's advisor	English
Ricardo	Rich and powerful ruler	Spanish
Riccardo	Rich and powerful ruler	Spanish
Rich	Rich and powerful ruler	English
Richard	Rich and powerful ruler	English
Richmond	Rich and powerful ruler	German
Rickard	Rich and powerful ruler	Scandinavian
Rico	Rich and powerful ruler	Spanish
Rikard	Rich and powerful ruler	German
Riocard	Rich and powerful ruler	Unknown
Risteard	Rich and powerful ruler	Unknown
Ritter	Chivalrous	German
Roald	Famous ruler	Norwegian
Rob	Bright with fame	English

Robb	Bright with fame	English
Robbie	Bright with fame	English
Robby	Bright with fame	English
Robert	Bright with fame	English
Roch	Glory	German
Rod	Famous ruler	English
Rodd	Famous ruler	English
Roddric	Famous ruler	German
Roddrick	Famous ruler	German
Roddy	Famous ruler	English
Roderic	Famous ruler	German
Roderick	Famous ruler	German
Roderik	Famous ruler	German
Rodrik	Famous ruler	German
Roger	Famous warrior	German
Roland	Famous in the land	German
Rolando	Famous in the land	Spanish
Rolf	Wolf counsel	German
Rollan	Famous in the land	German
Rolland	Famous in the land	German
Rollie	Famous in the land	German
Rollo	Famous in the land	German
Ross	Red haired	French
Rossiter	Red	French
Rosston	Red	French
Rosswald	Field of roses	English

Roswald	Field of roses	English
Roswalt	Field of roses	English
Roswell	Field of roses	English
Roth	Red haired	German
Rowland	Famous in the land	German
Royce	Son of Roy	English
Rudiger	Famous spearman	German
Rudy	Famous wolf	English
Rune	Secret	German
Ruodrik	Famous ruler	Unknown
Rupert	Bright fame	German
Ruprecht	Bright fame	German
Rutger	Famous spearman	Dutch
Ryszard	Powerful ruler	Unknown
Saelac	Blessed	Unknown
Schaeffer	Shepherd	German
Schaffer	Shepherd	German
Selig	Blessed	German
Selik	Blessed	German
Sherman	Shearman	English
Shermon	Shearman	English
Siegfried	Victorious	German
Siegmund	Victorious protection	German
Sigfrid	Victorious	German
Sigifrid	Victorious	German
Sigifrith	Victorious	German
Sigiwald	Victorious protector	German
Sigmund	Victorious protector	Old Norse

Sigmund	Victorious protection	German
Sigwald	Victorious protector	German
Sigwalt	Victorious protector	German
Silvester	Forest dweller	Latin
Spangler	Tinsmith	German
Spengler	Tinsmith	German
Stefan	Crowned or crown of laurels	German
Stein	Stone	German
Steiner	Stone	German
Sterling	Of high quality or pure	Old English
Sterlyn	Of high quality or pure	English
Stirling	Of high quality or pure	English
Tab	Brilliant	German
Tabbart	Brilliant	German
Tahbert	Brilliant	German
Tavin	Staff of the Goths	Scandinavian
Tedrick	Ruler of the people	American
Terell	Thunder ruler	German
Terrall	Thunder ruler	German
Terrel	Thunder ruler	German
Terrell	Thunder ruler	German

Terrelle	Thunder ruler	German
Terrill	Thunder ruler	German
Tihalt	Prince of the people	Unknown
Treffen	Meets	Unknown
Trennen	Divides	Unknown
Tretan	Walks	Unknown
Ubel	Evil	German
Uli	Noble leader	German
Ulrich	World ruler	German
Ulz	Noble leader	German
Valdemar	Famous ruler	Scandinavian
Valdemarr	Famous ruler	Scandinavian
Vemados	Courage of a bear	Unknown
Volker	People's guard	German
Volney	People's spirit	German
Volny	People's spirit	German
Von	Dyke	German
Wagner	Wagon maker	German
Waldemar	Famous ruler	German
Waldemarr	Famous ruler	German
Walden	Wooded valley	English
Waldhramm	Ruling raven	German
Waldifrid	Peaceful ruler	German
Waldmunt	Mighty protector	German
Waldo	God's power	German
Waldrom	Ruler	English
Waldron	Ruler	English

Walfred	Peaceful ruler	German
Walfrid	Peaceful ruler	German
Wallace	From Wales	English
Wallache	From Wales	English
Waller	Army ruler	German
Wally	Army ruler	German
Walmond	Mighty protector	German
Walt	Army ruler	German
Walten	Army ruler	German
Walter	Army ruler	German
Walthari	Army ruler	German
Walton	Walled town	English
Waren	Loyal	German
Warenhari	Armed defender	German
Warner	Armed defender	German
Warren	Loyal	German
Webber	Weaver	German
Weber	Weaver	German
Wendale	Traveler or wanderer	German
Wendall	Traveler or wanderer	German
Wendel	Traveler or wanderer	German
Wendell	Traveler or wanderer	German
Werner	Armed defender or defending army	English
Wilbart	Resolute	Unknown
Wilber	Resolute	English
Wilbert	Resolute	German

Wilbur	Walled stronghold	Old English
Wilburn	Resolute	English
Wilburt	Resolute	English
Wilford	Willow tree ford	English
Wilfred	Resolute protector	German
Wilfredo	Resolute protector	Spanish
Wilfrid	Resolute or peaceful	German
Wilhelm	Resolute protector	German
Willamar	Resolute or famous	German
Willaperht	Resolute or brilliant	German
Willard	Bold or resolute	German
William	Resolute protector	German
Williamon	Resolute protector	German
Williams	Resolute protector	German
Willifrid	Resolute or peaceful	German
Willimod	Resolute spirit	German
Willis	Resolute protector	German
Willmar	Resolute or famous	German
Willmarr	Resolute or famous	German
Wilmar	Resolute or famous	German
Wilmer	Resolute or	German

	famous	
Wilmod	Resolute spirit	German
Wilmot	Resolute spirit	German
Wilpert	Resolute or brilliant	German
Windell	Traveler or wanderer	English
Wolfgang	Advancing wolf	German
Wolfric	Wolf ruler	German
Wolfrick	Wolf ruler	German
Wolfrik	Wolf ruler	German
Xiomar	Famous in battle	Unknown
Zacharia	God remembers	Hebrew
Zelig	Happy	Hebrew

Greek

Greek names are among some of the most beautiful in the world. They descend from Greek mythology, history, and philosophy – from the mouths and pens of Socrates and Homer, and represented by some of the best men and women the world has to offer. Greek names are as traditional, beautiful, and unique as Greece itself. Think of names like Achilles, Diana, and even Eurydice when naming your child.

GIRLS	MEANING	ORIGIN
Adonia	Attractive	Greek
Agalia	Gaiety or joy	Greek
Agathe	Honorable or good	Greek
Akilina	Little eagle	Russian
Aleka	Defender of	Greek

	mankind	
Alethea	Truth	Greek
Alethia	Truth	Greek
Alithea	Truth	Greek
Anastasia	Resurrection	Greek
Andrianna	Manly	Greek
Angele	Messenger	Greek
Angeliki	Angelic or messenger	Greek
Antheia	Flowery	Greek
Antonia	Priceless, inestimable or praiseworthy	Latin
Arete	War	Greek
Artemisia	Perfection	Greek
Aspasia	Welcome	Greek
Athanasia	Immortal	Greek
Athena	Skill or wisdom	Greek
Baptista	A baptizer	Latin
Berdine	Glorious and famous maiden	German
Calandra	Lark	Greek
Calantha	Beautiful flower	Greek
Calida	Most beautiful	Latin
Calla	Beautiful	Greek
Callia	Beautiful voice	Greek
Callista	She that is most beautiful	Greek
Candace	Pure or glowing	Latin
Cass	Helper of men	Greek
Cassia	Cinnamon	Greek
Charis	Charity grace or kindness	Greek
Charissa	Charity grace or kindness	Greek
Chloris	Pale	Greek
Cleopatra	Her father's fame	Greek

Clio	Glorifier	Greek
Cloris	Pale	Greek
Cosima	Order or harmony	Greek
Cyma	Swollen	Greek
Damara	Gentle	Greek
Damaris	Gentle	Greek
Damia	To tame	Greek
Daphne	Laurel	Greek
Daphney	Laurel	Greek
Delfina	Dolphin	Greek
Delia	Visible	Greek
Delphina	Dolphin	Greek
Delphine	Dolphin	Greek
Delphinia	Dolphin	Greek
Demetra	Of the earth	Greek
Demetria	Of the earth	Greek
Dimitra	Of the earth	Greek
Dimitria	Of the earth	Greek
Diona	Divine	Greek
Dione	Divine	Greek
Dionis	Divine	Greek
Dionne	Divine	Greek
Dominica	Belonging to the Lord	Latin
Dora	Gift	Greek
Dorcus	Gazelle	Greek
Doria	Of the sea	Greek
Dorice	Of the sea	Greek
Dorise	Of the sea	Greek
Dorris	Of the sea	Greek
Dorrise	Of the sea	Greek
Dorthea	Gift of God	Greek
Drucilla	The strong one	Latin
Drusilla	The strong one	Latin
Elaine	Light	French
Electra	Shining	Greek

Eleftheria	Freedom or liberty	Greek
Elena	Light	Greek
Eleni	Light	English
Elenitsa	Light	Greek
Ellena	Light	English
Elpida	Hope	Greek
Erianthe	Sweet flowers	Greek
Euphemia	Fair of voice	Greek
Evangelia	Bringer of good news	Latin
Evangeline	Bringer of good news	Greek
Evania	Bringer of good news	Greek
Evanthe	Fair flower	Greek
Filia	Daughter	Latin
Galatea	Ivory colored	Greek
Helena	Light	Greek
Helia	The sun	Greek
Hera	Protectress	Greek
Hermione	Messenger	Greek
Hesper	Evening star	Greek
Ianthe	Purple flower	Greek
Io	Heifer	Greek
Ioanna	God is gracious	Greek
Iona	Violet	Greek
Ione	Violet	Greek
Ionia	Violet	Greek
Iphigeneia	Born royal	Greek
Isaura	From Isauria	Greek
Jocasta	Unknown	Greek
Junia	Unknown	Greek
Justina	Just	Latin
Kali	Flower bud	Greek
Kalika	Flower bud	Greek
Kalliope	Beautiful voice	Greek

Kalonice	Beautiful victory	Greek
Kaly	Flower bud	Greek
Kalyca	Flower bud	Greek
Kora	Maiden	Greek
Koren	Maiden	Greek
Kynthia	Moon	Greek
Lalage	Talkative	Greek
Lana	Wool	Latin
Leda	Lady	Greek
Lena	Light	Greek
Lia	Bringer of good news	Greek
Ligia	To select	Latin
Lilika	Lily	Latin
Litsa	Bringer of good news	Latin
Lucia	Bringer of light	Italian
Malaina	Dark or black	Greek
Malantha	Dark flower	Greek
Mara	Eternally beautiful	Greek
Marina	Sea maiden	Latin
Maris	Of the sea	Latin
Melania	Dark or black	Greek
Melantha	Dark flower	Greek
Melina	Canary yellow	Latin
Nani	Gracious	Greek
Nerissa	Sea nymph	Greek
Nike	Victory	Greek
Nikoleta	Victory of the people	Greek
Niobe	Unknown	Greek
Nitsa	Light	Greek
Nysa	Begining	Greek
Nyssa	Begining	Greek
Odele	Song	Greek
Pandora	Highly gifted	Greek

Pangiota	Very holy	Greek
Panthea	Of every God	Greek
Parthenie	A maiden	Greek
Pelagia	The sea	Greek
Petrina	A rock	Greek
Phaedra	Unknown	Greek
Philothea	Loving God	Greek
Rena	Peace	Greek
Rhea	Flowing	Greek
Rhode	Rose	Greek
Ritsa	Defender of mankind	Greek
Salome	Peace	Hebrew
Sibyl	Prophetess	Greek
Sofronia	Wisdom	Greek
Sophia	Wisdom	Greek
Stefania	Crowned or crown of laurels	Greek
Syma	Swollen	Greek
Tatiana	Fairy princess	Russian
Tessa	Harvester	Greek
Thea	Flowery	Greek
Thekla	Divine glory	Greek
Theodora	God's gift	Greek
Theodosia	Gift from God	Greek
Theophania	God has appeared	Greek
Theophilia	God's love	Greek
Thetis	Disposed	Greek
Timothea	One who honors God	English
Vanessa	Butterfly	Greek
Varvara	Foreign woman	Russian
Xenia	Hospitable	Greek
Zena	Hospitable	Greek
Zephyra	West wind	Greek
Zoe	Life	Greek

BOYS	MEANING	ORIGIN
Achillios	Unknown	Greek
Adonis	Handsome	Greek
Agapios	Love	Greek
Alekos	Defender of mankind	Greek
Alexandros	Defender of mankind	Greek
Alexios	Defender of mankind	Greek
Altair	Star	Greek
Anastasios	Resurrection	Greek
Anatolios	From the east	Greek
Apollo	Manly	Greek
Apolo	Manly	Greek
Argus	Watchful	Greek
Aristides	Best	Greek
Aristokles	Most famous	Greek
Aristotelis	Seeking the best	Greek
Aristotle	Seeking the best	Greek
Arsenios	Masculine	Greek
Athanasios	Immortal	Greek
Augustine	Majestic	Latin
Baltsaros	Prince of splendor	Greek
Baruch	Blessed	Hebrew
Basil	Kingly	Latin
Benedictus	Blessed	Latin
Carolos	Manly	Greek
Christiano	Follower of Christ or anointed	Italian
Christophoros	Christ bearer	Greek
Christos	Christ bearer	Greek
Claudios	Lame	Latin
Cletus	Illustrious	Greek
Constantinos	Constant or steadfast	Latin

Costa	Constant or steadfast	Greek
Damaskenos	Of Damascus	Greek
Damaskinos	Of Damascus	Greek
Damaskos	Of Damascus	Greek
Damianos	To tame	Greek
Demetios	Of the earth	Greek
Demetri	Of the earth	Greek
Demetrius	Of the earth	Greek
Denys	God of wine	French
Dhimitrios	Of Demeter	Greek
Dinos	God of wine	Greek
Dion	God of wine	Greek
Dionysios	God of wine	Greek
Eleftherios	Freedom or liberty	Greek
Eleutherios	Freedom or liberty	Greek
Elias	Jehovah is God	Hebrew
Erasmus	Lovable	Greek
Eugen	Well born or noble	German
Eugenios	Well born or noble	Greek
Eusebios	Venerable	Greek
Felix	Fortunate or happy	Latin
Flavian	Blond or fair haired	Latin
Georgios	Farmer	Greek
Giannes	God is gracious	Greek
Gregor	Vigilant watchman	Greek
Gregorios	Vigilant watchman	Greek
Hali	The sea	Greek
Hemeros	A pledge	Greek
Heraklees	Divine glory	Greek

Herakles	Divine glory	Greek
Hesperos	Evening star	Greek
Hieremias	The Lord will uplift	Greek
Hieronymos	Holy name	Greek
Hippolytus	Freer of horses	Greek
Iakovos	Supplanter	Greek
Ignatios	Fiery or ardent	Latin
Ioannes	God is gracious	Greek
Iorgos	Farmer	Greek
Isaakios	Laughter	Greek
Isadorios	Gift of Isis	Greek
Isidore	Gift of Isis	Greek
Jannes	God is gracious	Scandinavian
Joacheim	God shall establish	Hebrew
Klemenis	Merciful	Latin
Kristos	The anointed	Greek
Kyros	Lordly	Greek
Laurentios	From Laurentum	Latin
Leandros	Lion man or brave as a lion	Greek
Leiandros	Lion man or brave as a lion	Greek
Leontios	Lion	Latin
Loukas	Bringer of light	Latin
Lucais	Bringer of light	Scottish
Lucian	Bringer of light	Latin
Lukas	Bringer of light	Latin
Lukianos	Bringer of light	Latin
Lysander	Defender of mankind	Greek
Mahail	Who is like God	Hebrew
Maichail	Who is like God	Hebrew
Makarios	Blessed	Greek
Marinos	Of the sea or sailor	Greek

Markos	Warlike	Latin
Matthaios	Gift from God	Greek
Matthias	Gift from God	Greek
Maximos	The greatest	Latin
Mikhail	Who is like God	Russian
Mikhalis	Who is like God	Greek
Mikhos	Who is like God	Greek
Milos	Favor	Greek
Mitros	Of Demeter	Greek
Mitsos	Of Demeter	Greek
Moris	Dark	Greek
Nannos	God is gracious	Greek
Nectarios	Nectar	Greek
Nestor	One who is departing	Greek
Nicodemus	Victory of the people	Greek
Nikolaos	Victory of the people	Greek
Nikolos	Victory of the people	Greek
Nikos	Victory of the people	Greek
Nilos	Victory of the people	Greek
Oreste	Mountain	Greek
Orestes	Mountain	Greek
Orion	Unknown	Greek
Parthenios	Of or like a virgin	Greek
Paulos	Small	Latin
Pavlos	Small	Latin
Pericles	Just fame	Greek
Petros	Rock	Greek
Philippos	Lover of horses	Greek
Prokopios	Progressive leader	Greek
Romanos	A Roman	Latin
Rouvin	Behold a son	Hebrew

Samouel	His name is God	Greek
Seraphim	To burn	Latin
Sergio	Attendant	Italian
Silas	Asked for	Latin
Silvanos	Forest dweller	Latin
Socrates	Wise	Greek
Soterios	Savior or deliverer	Greek
Spiridon	A round basket	Greek
Spyridon	A round basket	Greek
Stephenos	Garland that surrounds	Greek
Symeon	Heard	Hebrew
Thanasis	Immortal	Greek
Thanos	Immortal	Greek
Theodosios	Gift of God	Greek
Theophilus	Loved by God	Greek
Timotheos	One who honors God	Greek
Titos	To honor	Greek
Vasileios	King	Greek
Vasilios	King	Greek
Vasilis	King	Greek
Venedictos	Blessed	Latin
Vernandos	Strong as a bear	Greek
Verniamin	Son of the right hand	Greek
Yanni	God is gracious	Greek
Zachaios	Remember the Lord	Greek
Zacheus	Remember the Lord	Greek
Zeno	Harness	Greek
Zenon	Harness	Greek

Native American

The history of Native Americans seems to be disappearing on a daily basis, but a way to ensure people remember and honor the heritage is to name the next generation of movers and shakers after their ancestors. Native American names come from different tribes, and some are attributed to different tribes, but they are all beautiful and roll off of the tongue in a way so few names do. These names aren't just Pocahontas, but ones you wouldn't even think, like Anna and Abbey.

GIRLS	MEANING	ORIGIN
Abedabun	Sight of day	Chippewa
Abequa	She stays at home	Chippewa
Abeque	She stays at home	Chippewa
Abey	Leaf	Omaha
Abeytu	Green leaf	Omaha
Abeytzi	Yellow leaf	Omaha
Adoette	Large tree	Unknown
Adsila	Blossom	Cherokee
Aiyana	Eternal blossom	Unknown
Alameda	Grove of cottonwood	Unknown
Alaqua	Sweet gum tree	Unknown
Alawa	Pea	Algonquian
Aleshanee	She plays all the time	Coos
Algoma	Valley of flowers	Unknown
Alsoomse	Independent	Algonquian
Altsoba	All are at war	Navajo
Amadahy	Forest water	Cherokee
Amitola	Rainbow	Unknown
Anaba	She returns from war	Navajo
Anemy	Superior	Unknown
Angeni	Spirit	Unknown
Angpetu	Radiant	Sioux

Angwusnasomtaqa	Crow mother spirit	Hopi
Ankti	Repeat dance	Hopi
Anna	Mother	Algonquian
Aponi	Butterfly	Unknown
Aquene	Peace	Unknown
Atepa	Wigwam	Choctaw
Awanatu	Turtle	Miwok
Awenasa	My home	Cherokee
Awendela	Morning	Unknown
Awinita	Fawn	Cherokee
Ayasha	Little one	Chippewa
Ayashe	Little one	Chippewa
Ayita	First to dance	Cherokee
Bena	Pheasant	Unknown
Bly	Tall	Unknown
Catori	Spirit	Hopi
Cha'kwaina	One who cries	Hopi
Chapa	Beaver	Sioux
Chapawee	Industrious	Sioux
Cha'risa	Elk	Hopi
Chenoa	Dove	Unknown
Chepi	Fairy	Algonquian
Chilam	Snowbird	Unknown
Chimalis	Bluebird	Unknown
Chitsa	Fair	Unknown
Chochmingwu	Corn mother	Hopi
Cholena	Bird	Unknown
Chosovi	Bluebird	Hopi
Chosposi	Bluebird eye	Hopi
Chu'mana	Snake maiden	Hopi
Chumani	Dewdrops	Sioux
Chu'si	Snake flower	Hopi
Cocheta	Stranger	Unknown
Dena	Valley	Unknown
Doba	There was no war	Navajo

Doli	Bluebird	Navajo
Donoma	Visible sun	Omaha
Dowanhowee	Singing voice	Sioux
Dyani	Deer	Unknown
hawee	Laughing maid	Sioux
Elu	Beautiful	Zuni
Enola	Solitary	Unknown
Etenia	Rich	Unknown
Eyota	Great	Unknown
Fala	Crow	Choctaw
Flo	Arrow	Unknown
Gaho	Mother	Unknown
Galilahi	Attractive	Cherokee
Genesee	Beautiful valley	Iroquois
Hachi	Stream	Seminole
Haiwee	Dove	Shoshone
Hakidonmuya	Time of waiting	Hopi
Haloke	Salmon	Navajo
Halona	Of happy fortune	Unknown
Hantaywee	Faithful	Sioux
Hateya	To press with the foot	Miwok
Hausis	Old woman	Algonquian
Hausisse	Old woman	Algonquian
Hehewuti	Warrior mother spirit	Hopi
Helki	To touch	Miwok
Honovi	Strong deer	Hopi
Huata	To carry seeds	Miwok
Humita	Shelled corn	Hopi
Hurit	Beautiful	Algonquian
Huyana	Rain falling	Miwok
Imala	Disaplines	Unknown
Isi	Deer	Choctaw
Istas	Snow	Unknown
Ituha	Sturdy oak	Unknown

Izusa	White stone	Unknown
Kachina	Spirit	Hopi
Kai	Willow tree	Navajo
Kakawangwa	Bitter	Hopi
Kaliska	Coyote chasing deer	Miwok
Kanti	Sings	Algonquian
Kasa	Dressed in furs	Hopi
Kay	Elder sister	Hopi
Keegsquaw	Virgin	Algonquian
Keezheekoni	Fire Briskly burning	Chippewa
Kewanee	Prairie hen	Potawatomi
Kimama	Butterfly	Shoshone
Kimi	Secret	Algonquian
Kimimela	Butterfly	Sioux
Kineks	Rosebud	Unknown
Kiwidinok	Womanof the wind	Chippewa
Koko	Night	Blackfoot
Kokyangwuti	Spider woman at middle age	Hopi
Kuwanlelenta	To make beautiful surroundings	Hopi
Kuwanyamtiwa	Beautiful badger going over the hill	Hopi
Kuwanyauma	Butterfly showing beautiful wings	Hopi
Kwanita	God is gracious	Zuni
Lenmana	Flute girl	Hopi
Leotie	Flower of the prairie	Unknown
Litonya	Hummingbird darting	Miwok
Lomahongva	Beautiful clouds	Hopi

	arising	
Lomasi	Pretty flower	Unknown
Lulu	Rabbit	Unknown
Luyu	Wild dove	Unknown
Macha	Aurora	Sioux
Magaskawee	Swan maiden or graceful	Sioux
Magena	Moon	Unknown
Mahal	Woman	Unknown
Mai	Coyote	Unknown
Maka	Earth	Sioux
Makawee	Earth maiden or generous	Sioux
Makkitotosimew	She has large breasts	Algonquian
Malia	Bitter or sea of bitterness	Zuni
Malila	Salmon going fast up a rippling stream	Miwok
Manaba	War returned with her coming	Navajo
Mansi	Plucked flower	Hopi
Mapiya	Sky or heavenly	Sioux
Maralah	Born during an earthquake	Unknown
Mausi	Plucks flowers	Unknown
Meda	Prophetess	Unknown
Meli	Bitter	Zuni
Memdi	Henna	Unknown
Meoquanee	Wears red	Chippewa
Miakoda	Power of the moon	Unknown
Migina	Returning moon	Omaha
Migisi	Eagle	Chippewa
Mika	Intelligent raccoon	Sioux

Mimiteh	New moon	Omaha
Minal	Fruit	Unknown
Mitena	Born under coming or new moon	Omaha
Muna	Overflowing spring	Hopi
Nadie	Wise	Algonquian
Nahimana	Mystic	Sioux
Namid	Star dancing	Chippewa
Nara	From Nara	Unknown
Nascha	Owl	Navajo
Nashota	Twin	Unknown
Nata	Speaker	Unknown
Nijlon	Mistress	Algonquian
Nina	Strong	Unknown
Ninovan	Our home	Cheyenne
Nita	Bear	Choctaw
Nittawosew	She is not sterile	Algonquian
Nituna	Daughter	Unknown
Nokomis	Grandmother	Chippewa
Nova	Chases butterfly	Hopi
Nukpana	Evil	Hopi
Numees	Sister	Algonquian
Nuna	Land	Unknown
Nuttah	My heart	Algonquian
Odahingum	Rippling water	Chippewa
Odina	Mountain	Algonquian
Ogin	Wild rose	Unknown
Ojinjintka	Rose	Sioux
Olathe	Beautiful	Unknown
Ominotago	Pleasant voice	Chippewa
Omusa	Missing when shooting with arrows	Miwok
Onawa	Wide awake	Unknown
Onida	The one	Unknown

	searched for	
Oota dabun	Day star	Algonquian
Opa	Owl	Choctaw
Orenda	Magic power	Iroquois
Pakwa	Frog	Hopi
Pamuy	Water moon	Hopi
Papina	A vine growing on an oak tree	Miwok
Pati	Fish basket	Miwok
Pauwau	Witch	Algonquian
Pavati	Clear water	Hopi
Pazi	Yellow bird	Ponca
Pelipa	Lover of horses	Zuni
Peta	Golden eagle	Blackfoot
Petah	Golden eagle	Blackfoot
Petunia	Flower name	Unknown
Polikwaptiwa	Butterfly sitting on a flower	Hopi
Poloma	Bow	Choctaw
Posala	Farewell to spring flowers	Miwok
Powaqa	Witch	Hopi
Ptaysanwee	White buffalo	Sioux
Pules	Pigeon	Algonquian
Quanah	Fragrant	Comanche
Rozene	Rose	Unknow
Sahkyo	Mink	Navajo
Salali	Squirrel	Cherokee
Sapata	Dancing bear	Miwok
Shada	Pelican	Unknown
Sheshebens	Small duck	Chippewa
Shuman	Rattlesnake handler	Hopi
Sihu	Flower	Hopi
Sikya	Small canyon	Hopi
Sinopa	Kit fox	Blackfoot
Sipatu	Pulled out	Miwok

Sisika	Bird	Unknown
Sitala	Display memory	Miwok
Snana	Jingle like little bells	Sioux
Sokanon	Rain	Algonquian
Sokw	Sour	Algonquian
Sonoma	Ground place	Miwok
Sooleawa	Silver	Algonquian
Soyala	Time of the winter solstice	Hopi
Stinka	Magical dancer	Unknown
Suleta	To fly around	Miwok
Suni	Middle	Zuni
Sunki	To catch up with	Hopi
Taa	Seed	Zuni
Tablita	Crown	Hopi
Tadewi	Wind	Omaha
Tahki	Cold	Algonquian
Taima	Thunder	Unknown
Taini	New moon	Omaha
Taipa	Flying quail	Miwok
Takala	Corn tassel	Hopi
Tala	Wolf	Unknown
Talulah	Leaping water	Choctaw
Tama	Thunder	Unknown
Tansy	Name of a flower	Hopi
Tayanita	Young beaver	Cherokee
Tehya	Predous	Unknown
Tiponi	Child of importance	Hopi
Tis-see-woo-na-tis	She who bathes with her knees	Cheyenne
Tiva	Dance	Hopi
Tolikna	Coyote's long ears flapping	Miwok
Totsi	Moccasins	Hopi

Tusa	Prairie dog	Zuni
Tuuwa	Sand	Hopi
Tuwa	Earth	Hopi
Una	Remember	Hopi
Unega	White	Cherokee
Urika	Useful	Omaha
Usdi	Baby	Cherokee
Utina	Woman of my country	Timucua
Wachiwi	Dancing girl	Sioux
Waki	Shelter	Hopi
Waneta	Charger	Unknown
Wapun	Dawn	Potawatomi
Wawetseka	Pretty woman	Potawatomi
Weayaya	Sunset	Sioux
Wenona	Firstborn daughter	Unknown
Wicapi wakan	Holy star	Dakota
Wichahpi	Star	Sioux
Wikimak	Wife	Algonquian
Winema	Chief	Unknown
Winona	First born daughter	Sioux
Wuti	Woman	Hopi
Wyanet	Beautiful	Unknown
Wyome	Large plain	Algonquian
Yamka	Blossom	Hopi
Yanaba	She meets the enemy	Navajo
Yatokya	Sun	Zuni
Yenene	Medicine man	Miwok
Yepa	Snow woman	Unknown
Yoki	It rained	Hopi
Yona	Bear	Cherokee
Yutu	Coyote out hunting	Miwok
Zaltana	High mountain	Unknown

Zihna	Spins	Hopi
Ziracuny	Water monster	Kiowa
Zitkala	Bird	Dakota
Zonta	Trustworthy	Sioux
BOYS	**MEANING**	**ORIGIN**
Abooksigun	Wildcat	Algonquian
Abukcheech	Mouse	Algonquian
Achachak	Spirit	Algonquian
Achak	Spirit	Algonquian
Adahy	Lives in the woods	Cherokee
Adoeette	Great tree	Kiowa
Ahanu	He laughs	Algonquian
Ahiga	He fights	Navajo
Ahmik	Beaver	Chippewa
Ahote	Restless one	Hopi
Ahtunowhiho	One who lives below	Cheyenne
Akando	Ambush	Unknown
Akecheta	Fighter	Sioux
Akule	Looks up	Unknown
Alo	He looks up	Hopi
Anakausuen	Worker	Algonquian
Anoki	Actor	Unknown
Apenimon	Worthy of trust	Unknown
Apiatan	Wooden lance	Kiowa
Apisi	Coyote	Blackfoot
Aponivi	Where the wind blows down the gap	Hopi
Aranck	Stars	Algonquian
Ashkii	Boy	Navajo
Askook	Snake	Algonquian
Askuwheteau	He keeps watch	Algonquian
Ata'halne	He interrupts	Navajo
Atohi	Woods	Cherokee
Atsadi	Fish	Cherokee

Atsidi	Hammer	Navajo
Avonaco	Leaning bear	Cheyenne
Awan	Somebody	Unknown
Ayawamat	One who follows orders	Hopi
Bemossed	Walker	Unknown
Beshkno	Bald eagle	Potawatomi
Bidziil	He is strong	Navajo
Bilagaana	White person	Navajo
Bimisi	Slippery	Unknown
Bodaway	Fire maker	Unknown
Cha'akmongwi	Crier chief	Hopi
Chankoowashtay	Good road	Sioux
Chansomps	Locust	Algonquian
Chapa	Beaver	Sioux
Chas chunk a	Wave	Winnebago
Chatan	Hawk	Sioux
Cha'tima	The caller	Hopi
Chavatangakwunua	Short rainbow	Hopi
Chayton	Falcon	Sioux
Chesmu	Witty	Unknown
Cheveyo	Spirit warrior	Hopi
Chochmo	Mud mound	Hopi
Chochokpi	Throne for the clouds	Hopi
Chochuschuvio	White tailed deer	Hopi
Chogan	Blackbird	Algonquian
Choovio	Antelope	Hopi
Choviohoya	Young deer	Hopi
Chowilawu	Joined together by water	Hopi
Chu'a	Snake	Hopi
Chuchip	Deer spirit	Hopi
Chunta	Cheating	Hopi
Ciqala	Little one	Dakota
Cochise	Hardwood	Apache

Dakota	Allies or friends	Sioux
Dakotah	Allies or friends	Sioux
Degotoga	Standing together	Cherokee
Delsin	He is so	Unknown
Demothi	Talks while walking	Unknown
Dichali	Speaks a lot	Unknown
Diwali	Bowls	Cherokee
Dohate	Bluff	Kiowa
Dohosan	Little bluff	Kiowa
Dustu	Spring frog	Cherokee
Dyami	Eagle	Unknown
Elan	Friendly	Unknown
Elki	Hanging over the top	Miwok
Elsu	Soaring falcon	Miwok
Eluwilussit	Holy one	Algonquian
Enapay	Appears Bravely	Sioux
Enkoodabaoo	One who lives alone	Algonquian
Enyeto	Walks Like a bear	Miwok
Etchemin	Canoe man	Algonquian
Etlelooaat	Shouts	Algonquian
Etu	Sun	Unknown
Ezhno	Solitary	Unknown
Gaagii	Raven	Navajo
Gad	Juniper tree	Navajo
Gawonii	He is speaking	Cherokee
Gomda	Wind	Kiowa
Gosheven	Great leaper	Unknown
Guyapi	Candid	Unknown
Hahkethomemah	Little robe	Cheyenne
Hahnee	Beggar	Unknown
Hakan	Fire	Unknown
Halian	Youthful	Zuni

Hania	Spirit warrior	Hopi
Hanska	Tall	Sioux
Harkahome	Little robe	Cheyenne
Hassun	Stone	Algonquian
Hastiin	Man	Navajo
Hawiovi	Going down the ladder	Hopi
He lush ka	Fighter	Winnebago
Heammawihio	Wise one above	Cheyenne
Helaku	Sunny day	Unknown
Helki	To touch	Miwok
Heskovizenako	Porcupine bear	Cheyenne
Hesutu	Yellow jacket's nest rising from the ground	Miwok
Hevataneo	Hairyrope	Cheyenne
Hevovitastamiutsto	Whirlwind	Cheyenne
Hiamovi	High chief	Cheyenne
Hinto	Blue	Dakota
Hohnihohkaiyohos	High backed wolf	Cheyenne
Hok'ee	Abandoned	Navajo
Holata	Alligator	Seminole
Honani	Badger	Hopi
Honaw	Bear	Hopi
Honiahaka	Little wolf	Cheyenne
Honon	Bear	Miwok
Honovi	Strong	Hopi
Hotah	White	Sioux
Hototo	Warrior spirit who sings	Hopi
Hotuaekhaashtait	Tall bull	Cheyenne
Howahkan	Of the mysterious voice	Sioux
Howi	Turtle dove	Miwok
Huritt	Handsome	Algonquian
Igasho	Wanders	Unknown

Iiniwa	Bison or buffalo	Blackfoot
Illanipi	Amazing	Unknown
Inteus	Has no shame	Unknown
Istaqa	Coyote man	Hopi
Istu	Sugar	Unknown
Ituha	Sturdy oak	Unknown
Iye	Smoke	Unknown
Jacy	Moon	Unknown
Jolon	Valley of the dead oaks	Unknown
Kachada	White man	Hopi
Kaga	Chronicler	Unknown
Kajika	Walks without sound	Unknown
Kangee	Crow	Sioux
Kanuna	Bullfrog	Cherokee
Kele	Sparrow	Hopi
Keme	Thunder	Algonquian
Kesegowaase	Swift	Algonquian
Kestejoo	Slave	Algonquian
Kilchii	Red boy	Navajo
Kitchi	Brave	Algonquian
Kiyiya	Howling wolf	Yakima
Klah	Left handed	Navajo
Knoton	Wind	Unknown
Kohana	Swift	Sioux
Kohkahycumest	White crow or white antelope	Cheyenne
Koi	Panther	Choctaw
Kolichiyaw	Skunk	Hopi
Kosumi	Spear fisher	Miwok
Kotori	Screech owl spirit	Hopi
Kuckunniwi	Little wolf	Cheyenne
Kuruk	Bear	Pawnee
Kusinut	Horseless	Yakima
Kwahu	Eagle	Hopi

Kwatoko	Bird with big beak	Hopi
Lallo	Little boy	Kiowa
Langundo	Peaceful	Unknown
Lansa	Lance	Hopi
Lapu	Cedar bark	Hopi
Len	Flute	Hopi
Lena	Flute	Hopi
Lenno	Man	Unknown
Leyti	Shaped like an abalone shell	Miwok
Lise	Salmon's head rising above water	Miwok
Liwanu	Growling bear	Miwok
Lokni	Rain falls through the roof	Miwok
Lonan	Cloud	Zuni
Lonato	Flint	Unknown
Lootah	Red	Sioux
Lusio	Light	Zuni
Machakw	Horny toad	Hopi
Machk	Bear	Algonquian
Mahkah	Earth	Sioux
Mahpee	Sky	Sioux
Makkapitew	He has large teeth	Algonquian
Makya	Eagle hunter	Hopi
Mammedaty	Walking above	Kiowa
Mantotohpa	Four bears	Cheyenne
Masichuvio	Gray deer	Hopi
Maska	Strong	Unknown
Matchitehew	He has an evil heart	Algonquian
Matchitisiw	He has bad character	Algonquian
Mato	Bear	Sioux

Matoskah	White bear	Sioux
Matunaagd	Fights	Algonquian
Matwau	Enemy	Algonquian
Maza blaska	Flat iron	Dakota
Megedagik	Kills many	Algonquian
Mekledoodum	Conceited	Algonquian
Meturato	Black kettle	Cheyenne
Micco	Chief	Seminole
Mika	Racoon	Sioux
Mikasi	Coyote	Omaha
Milap	Charitable	Unknown
Minco	Chief	Choctaw
Mingan	Gray wolf	Algonquian
Minninnewah	Whirlwind	Cheyenne
Misu	Rippling water	Miwok
Mochni	Talking bird	Hopi
Mohe	Elk	Cheyenne
Mojag	Never silent	Unknown
Mokatavatah	Black kettle	Cheyenne
Moketavato	Black kettle	Cheyenne
Moketaveto	Black kettle	Cheyenne
Moketoveto	Black kettle	Cheyenne
Moki	Deer	Hopi
Mokovaoto	Black kettle	Cheyenne
Molimo	Bear walking into shade	Miwok
Mongwau	Owl	Hopi
Motavato	Black kettle	Cheyenne
Motega	New arrow	Unknown
Muata	Yellow jackets inside a nest	Miwok
Mukki	Child	Algonquian
Muraco	White moon	Unknown
Naalnish	He works	Navajo
Naalyehe ya sidahi	Trader	Navajo
Nahcomence	Oldbark antelope	Cheyenne

Nahiossi	Has three fingers	Cheyenne
Nakai	Mexican	Navajo
Napayshni	Courageous	Sioux
Nashashuk	Thundering	Sauk
Nashoba	Wolf	Choctaw
Nastas	Curve like foxtail grass	Navajo
Nawat	Left handed	Unknown
Nawkaw	Wood	Winnebago
Nayati	He who wrestles	Unknown
Nayavu	Clay	Hopi
Neeheeoeewootis	High backed wolf	Cheyenne
Neka	Wild goose	Unknown
Nigan	Ahead	Unknown
Niichaad	Swollen	Navajo
Nikan	My friend	Potawatomi
Nikiti	Round or smooth	Unknown
Nitis	Friend	Unknown
Nixkamich	Grandfather	Algonquian
Niyol	Wind	Navajo
Nodin	Wind	Unknown
Nokosi	Bear	Seminole
Nootau	Fire	Algonquian
Nosh	Father	Algonquian
Noshi	Father	Algonquian
Notaku	Growling bear	Miwok
Nukpana	Evil	Hopi
Ocumwhowurst	Yellow wolf	Cheyenne
Ocunnowhurst	Yellow wolf	Cheyenne
Odakotah	Friendship	Sioux
Ogaleesha	Wears a red shirt	Sioux
Ogima	Chief	Potawatomi
Ogleesha	Red skirt	Sioux

Ohanko	Reckless	Unknown
Ohanzee	Shadow	Sioux
Ohcumgache	Little wolf	Cheyenne
Ohitekah	Brave	Sioux
Ohiyesa	Winner	Sioux
Okhmhaka	Little wolf	Cheyenne
Omawnakw	Cloud feather	Hopi
Onacona	White owl	Cherokee
Osceola	Black drink	Seminole
Otaktay	Kills many	Sioux
Otetiani	He is prepared	Iroquois
Otoahhastis	Tall bull	Cheyenne
Otoahnacto	Bull bear	Cheyenne
Ouray	Arrow	Unknown
Pachu'a	Feathered water snake	Hopi
Paco	Eagle	Unknown
Pahana	Lost white brother	Hopi
Pallaton	Warrior	Unknown
Pannoowau	He lies	Algonquian
Pat	Fish	Unknown
Patamon	Tempest	Unknown
Patwin	Man	Unknown
Pay	He is coming	Unknown
Payat	He is coming	Unknown
Payatt	He is coming	Unknown
Paytah	Fire	Sioux
Peopeo	Bird	Nez Perce
Pezi	Grass	Sioux
Pimne	Weasel	Hopi
Pitalesharo	Chief of men	Pawnee
Powwaw	Priest	Algonquian
Qaletaqa	Guardian of the people	Hopi
Qochata	White man	Hopi
Quanah	Fragrant	Comanche

Rowtag	Fire	Algonquian
Sahale	Falcon	Unknown
Sahkonteic	White eagle	Nez Perce
Sakima	Chief	Ojibwa
Samoset	He walks over much	Algonquian
Sani	The old one	Navajo
Satanta	White bear	Kiowa
Segenam	Lazy	Algonquian
Setangya	Sitting bear	Kiowa
Setimika	Charging bear	Kiowa
Sewati	Curved bear claw	Miwok
Shappa	Red thunder	Sioux
Shilah	Brother	Navajo
Shiriki	Coyote	Pawnee
Shiye	Son	Navajo
Shizhe'e	Father	Navajo
Shoemowetochawcawe	High backed wolf	Cheyenne
Sicheii	Grandfather	Navajo
Sike	He sits at home	Navajo
Sik'is	Friend	Navajo
Sikyahonaw	Yellow bear	Hopi
Sikyatavo	Yellow rabbit	Hopi
Sipatu	Pulled out	Miwok
Siwili	Long tail of the fox	Unknown
Skah	White	Sioux
Songaa	Strong	Unknown
Sowi'ngwa	Black tailed deer	Hopi
Sucki	Black	Algonquian
Sunukkuhkau	He crushes	Algonquian
Tadi	Wind	Omaha
Tadzi	Loon	Carrier
Tahkeome	Little robe	Cheyenne
Tahmelapachme	Dull knife	Cheyenne

Taima	Thunder	Unknown
Takoda	Friend to everyone	Sioux
Tangakwunu	Rainbow	Hopi
Tapco	Antelope	Kiowa
Tashunka	Horse	Sioux
Tasunke	Horse	Dakota
Tatanka ptecila	Short bull	Dakota
Tatonga	Large dear	Sioux
Tawa	Sun	Hopi
Teetonka	Big lodge	Sioux
Teluhci	Bear making dust	Miwok
Telutci	Bear making dust	Miwok
Tihkoosue	Short	Algonquian
T'iis	Cottonwood	Navajo
Tocho	Mountain lion	Hopi
Togquos	Twin	Algonquian
Tohopka	Wild beast	Hopi
Tokala	Fox	Dakota
Tooantuh	Spring frog	Cherokee
Tse	Rock	Navajo
Tsiishch'ili	Curly haired	Navajo
Tsiyi	Canoe	Cherokee
Tuari	Young eagle	Laguna
Tuketu	Bear making dust	Miwok
Tumu	Deer thinking of eating wild onions	Miwok
Tupi	To pull up	Miwok
Tyee	Chief	Chinook
Unaduti	Woolly head	Cherokee
Uzumati	Grizzly bear	Miwok
Vaiveahtoish	Alights on the cloud	Cheyenne
Viho	Chief	Cheyenne

Vipponah	Slim face	Cheyenne
Vohkinne	Roman nose	Cheyenne
Voistitoevitz	White cow	Cheyenne
Voisttitoevetz	White cow	Cheyenne
Vokivocummast	White antelope	Cheyenne
Waban	East wind	Algonquian
Wahanassatta	He who walks with his toes turned outward	Cheyenne
Wahchinksapa	Wise	Sioux
Wahchintonka	Has much Practice	Sioux
Wahkan	Sacred	Sioux
Wahkoowah	Charging bear	Sioux
Wakiza	Desperate warrior	Unknown
Wamblee	Eagle	Sioux
Wambleesha	White eagle	Sioux
Wambli waste	Good eagle	Dakota
Wanageeska	White spirit	Sioux
Wanahton	Charger	Sioux
Wanikiy	Savior	Sioux
Wapi	Lucky	Sioux
Waquini	Hook nose	Cheyenne
Weayaya	Setting sun	Sioux
Wematin	Brother	Algonquian
Wemilat	Of wealthy parents	Unknown
Wicasa	Sage	Dakota
Wikvaya	One who brings	Hopi
Wilu	Chicken hawk squawking	Miwok
Wohehiv	Dull knife	Cheyenne
Wokaihwokomas	White antelope	Cheyenne
Wuliton	To do well	Unknown
Wuyi	Soaring turkey vulture	Miwok

Wynono	First born	Unknown
Yaholo	Crier	Creek
Yahto	Blue	Sioux
Yancy	Englishman	Unknown
Yanisin	Ashamed	Navajo
Yas	Snow	Navajo
Yiska	The night has passed	Navajo
Yuma	Chiefs son	Unknown

Spanish

Spanish is one of the fastest growing languages in the world in terms of usage and learning, and Spanish names have been influencing parents more and more. It can open doors to multiculturalism, and awaken interest for heritage. There are Spanish names that you find every day, along with more exotic and traditional options that can offer the flair to make someone special. Look for something unique, but still easy enough for less trained tongues to pronounce!

GIRLS	MEANING	ORIGIN
Acacia	Thorny	Greek
Adalia	Of the nobility	Spanish
Adana	Of the red earth	Spanish
Adelina	Noble	English
Adelita	Noble	German
Adella	Noble	German
Adonia	Beautiful lady	Spanish
Adoracion	Adoration	Spanish
Adriana	Dark	Italian
Agacia	Kind	Greek
Agata	Kind	Greek
Agnese	Pure	Greek
Agueda	Kind	Greek
Aida	Helpful	Latin
Aidia	Help	Spanish
Aintzane	Glorious	Unknown
Alameda	Poplar tree	Spanish
Alandra	Defender of mankind	Spanish
Alanza	Ready for battle	Spanish

Alazne	Miracle	Unknown
Albertine	Noble	French
Alda	Old or wise	German
Aldene	Wise	German
Aldona	Wise	German
Aldonsa	Nice	Spanish
Aldonza	Nice	Spanish
Aleece	Of the nobility	German
Alegria	Cheerful or Happy	Latin
Alejandra	Defender of mankind	Spanish
Alejandrina	Defender of mankind	Spanish
Aleta	Winged	Greek
Aletea	Honest	Greek
Aletia	Honest	Greek
Alfonsa	Noble	Unknown
Alfreda	Wise counselor	Old English
Alhertina	Noble	Unknown
Alicia	Truthful	English
Alisa	Of the nobility	Greek
Alise	Of the nobility	Greek
Alita	Winged	Spanish
Alliss	Of the nobility	German
Allyce	Of the nobility	German
Alma	Soul	Latin
Almira	From Almeira	Spanish
Almunda	Refers to the Virgin Mary	Spanish
Almundena	Refers to the Virgin Mary	Spanish

Almundina	Refers to the Virgin Mary	Spanish
Aloise	Famous warrior or famous in battle	German
Alona	Light	Unknown
Alondra	Defender of mankind	Greek
Alonsa	Eager for battle	English
Alta	High	Latin
Altagracia	High	Spanish
Alvarita	Speaker of truth	Spanish
Alvera	Speaker of truth	Unknown
Alyce	Of the nobility	German
Alys	Of the nobility	German
Alyss	Of the nobility	German
Amada	To love God	Spanish
Amadia	Beloved	Spanish
Amalia	Industrious	German
Amalur	Homeland	Unknown
Amalure	Homeland	Unknown
Amanda	Lovable, worthy to be loved	Latin
Amara	Eternally beautiful	Greek
Amaranta	Flower that never fades	Spanish
Amaris	Given by God	Hebrew
Amarissa	Given by God	Hebrew

Amata	Lovable or dearly loved	Latin
Amedia	Beloved	Spanish
Amor	Love	Spanish
Amora	Love	Spanish
Ana	Grace	Spanish
Analee	Grace	English
Analeigh	Grace	English
Analena	Grace	Spanish
Anamarie	Grace or bitter	English
Anarosa	Grace	English
Andeana	Leaving	Spanish
Andera	Manly	Greek
Andere	Manly	Greek
Andrea	Manly	Greek
Andria	Manly	English
Angela	Messenger	Latin
Angelia	Angel	Spanish
Angelina	Messenger of God	English
Anica	Grace	Czech
Anita	Grace	Spanish
Anitia	Grace	Spanish
Anjelica	Like an angel	Greek
Anna	Grace	Hebrew
Antonia	Priceless, inestimable or praiseworthy	Latin
Antonina	Priceless, inestimable or praiseworthy	Latin
Anunciacion	To announce	Spanish
Aquilina	Eagle	Latin
Araceli	Altar of heaven	Latin

128

Aracelia	Altar of heaven	Latin
Aracely	Altar of heaven	Latin
Arama	Reference to the Virgin Mary	Unknown
Arcadia	Adventurous	Latin
Arcelia	Treasure	Latin
Arcilla	Altar of heaven	Latin
Arella	Messenger	Hebrew
Aricela	Altar of heaven	Latin
Ariela	Lion of God	Hebrew
Armanda	Noble	Latin
Artemisia	Perfection	Greek
Ascencion	To ascend	Spanish
Asuncion	Feast of the Assumption	Spanish
Atalaya	Guardtower	Unknown
Athalia	Guardtower	Unknown
Aurelia	Gold	Latin
Aureliana	Golden	Latin
Aurkena	Present	Unknown
Aurkene	Present	
Barbara	Foreign or stranger	Latin
Beatrisa	She who brings happiness	Spanish
Beatriz	She who brings happiness	Spanish
Belen	Bethlehem	Unknown
Belinda	Pretty or very beautiful	Spanish
Bella	Beautiful	Latin

Benigna	Kind	Spanish
Benita	Blessed	Spanish
Bernicia	One who brings victory	Greek
Berta	Bright or illustrious	Spanish
Bibiana	Lively	Latin
Bienvenida	Welcome	Spanish
Blanca	White	Italian
Blandina	Flattering	Latin
Blasa	Stammerer	French
Bonita	Pretty little one	Spanish
Breezy	Wind	Unknown
Brigidia	Strong	Celtic
Brisa	Beloved	Greek
Brisha	Beloved	Greek
Brisia	Beloved	Greek
Brissa	Beloved	Greek
Briza	Beloved	Greek
Bryssa	Beloved	Greek
Buena	Good	Spanish
Calandria	Lark	Greek
Calida	Ardent	Spanish
Calvina	Bald	Latin
Camila	Young ceremonial attendant	Spanish
Candi	Pure or glowing	American
Candida	Pure or bright white	Latin
Candie	Pure or glowing	American
Cari	Dear	Unknown
Carilla	Manly	Latin
Carisa	Beloved	Greek
Carla	Little and	English

	womanly	
Carletta	Little and womanly	Spanish
Carlita	Little and womanly	Spanish
Carlota	Little and womanly	Italian
Carlotta	Little and womanly	Italian
Carmela	Garden or vineyard	Hebrew
Carmelita	Garden or vineyard	Spanish
Carmen	Song	Latin
Carmencita	Song	Spanish
Carmina	Song	Spanish
Carmita	Song	Spanish
Carola	Song of joy	French
Carolina	Little and womanly	Italian
Carona	Crowned	Unknown
Carrola	Song of joy	French
Casandra	Doom	Greek
Casey	Brave	Irish
Casta	Pure	Greek
Catalina	Pure	Spanish
Cecilia	Dim sighted or blind	Latin
Celesta	Heavenly	English
Celestina	Heavenly	Spanish
Cenobia	Stranger	Greek
Ceri	Lordly	Greek
Ceria	Cherry or cherry red	Greek
Cesara	Long haired	Latin
Chalina	Form of Rosa	Spanish
Charo	Rosary	Spanish
Chavela	Consecrated	Spanish

	to God	
Chavelle	Consecrated to God	Spanish
Chaya	Life	Hebrew
Chela	Consolation	Spanish
Chica	Little girl	Spanish
Chiquita	Little girl	Spanish
Chrisanna	Variant of Chrysantus	English
Chrisanne	Variant of Chrysantus	English
Chrysann	Variant of Chrysantus	English
Cipriana	From Cyprus	Greek
Cira	Ladylike	Spanish
Ciri	Ladylike	Greek
Clara	Bright or clear	Latin
Clareta	Brilliant	Spanish
Clarinda	Bright or clear	Spanish
Clarisa	Bright or clear	Italian
Clarissa	Bright or clear	Italian
Claudia	Lame	Latin
Clementina	Merciful	Latin
Clodovea	Famous warrior	Unknown
Coco	Coconut	Spanish
Coleta	Victory of the people	French
Concepcion	Conception	Spanish
Concetta	Pure	Italian
Conchetta	Immaculate conception	Italian
Conchita	Immaculate conception	Spanish

Conshita	Conception	Spanish
Consolacion	Consolation	Spanish
Consolata	Consolation	Spanish
Constantia	Constant or steadfast	Latin
Constanza	Constant or steadfast	Italian/Spanish
Consuela	Consolation	Italian
Consuelo	Consolation	Spanish
Corazana	Heart	Spanish
Corazon	Heart	Spanish
Covadonga	First major victory for independency of Spain, 711 AD	Latin
Crisann	Variant of Chrysantus	English
Crisanna	Variant of Chrysantus	English
Crista	Follower of Christ or anointed	Italian
Cristina	Follower of Christ or anointed	Greek
Cristine	Follower of Christ or anointed	Greek
Cyntia	Moon	Spanish
Dalila	Delicate	Hebrew
Damita	Little noble	Spanish
Dani	God is my judge	Hebrew
Daniela	God is my judge	Spanish
Danita	God is my judge	Spanish
Daria	Rich or	Greek

	wealthy	
Delcine	Sweet	Unknown
Delfina	Dolphin	Greek
Delicia	Charming or delightful	English
Delma	Noble protector	Unknown
Delmar	Of the sea	Latin
Delmara	Of the sea	Latin
Delphia	Dolphin	Spanish
Denisa	God of wine	Spanish
Desideria	Desired or longed for	French
Destina	Fate	Spanish
Devera	Task	Unknown
Dia	Divine	Latin
Diega	Supplanter	Spanish
Digna	Worthy	Latin
Dina	Avenged or vindicated	Hebrew
Dinora	Avenged or vindicated	Hebrew
Dionis	Divine	Greek
Dionisa	Divine	Greek
Dita	Rich gift	English
Dolores	Full of sorrows	Spanish
Dolorita	Full of sorrows	Spanish
Domenica	Belonging to the Lord	Latin
Dominga	Born on Sunday	Spanish
Dominica	Belonging to the Lord	Latin
Dona	Lady	Italian
Dorbeta	Reference to the Virgin	Unknown

	Mary	
Dorotea	Gift of God	Spanish
Doroteia	Gift of God	Spanish
Dreena	Defender of mankind	Greek
Drina	Defender of mankind	Greek
Duena	Chaperon	Unknown
Dukine	Sweet	Unknown
Dukinea	Sweet	Unknown
Dulce	Sweet	Spanish
Dulcina	Sweet	Spanish
Dulcinea	Sweet	Spanish
Dulcinia	Sweet	Spanish
Earlena	Noblewoman	English
Earlene	Noblewoman	English
Earlina	Noblewoman	English
Edenia	Delight	Spanish
Edita	Prosperous in war	Spanish
Elbertina	Noble	Old English
Eldora	Gilded or Golden	Spanish
Eleadora	Gift of the sun	Spanish
Eleanora	Light	Greek
Eleena	Light	Greek
Elena	Light	Greek
Elina	Light	Greek
Elisa	God is my oath	Greek
Eloisa	Famous in war	French
Elsa	God is my oath	Hebrew
Elvera	Elfin	Old English
Elvira	Elfin	Spanish

Elvita	Truth	Spanish
Ema	Grandmother	German
Emilia	Industrious	Italian
Emilie	Industrious	English
Encarnacion	Incarnation of Christ	Spanish
Engracia	Graceful	Latin
Enrica	Ruler of the estate	Spanish
Enriqua	Ruler of the estate	Spanish
Enriqueta	Ruler of the estate	Spanish
Erendira	One with a smile	Spanish
Erendiria	One with a smile	Spanish
Erlene	Noblewoman	English
Erlina	Noblewoman	English
Ernesta	Sincere	English
Eskama	Merciful	Unknown
Eskame	Merciful	Unknown
Esma	Emerald	French
Esme	Emerald	French
Esmeralda	Emerald	Spanish
Esperanza	Hope	Spanish
Estebana	Crowned	Spanish
Estefana	Crowned	Spanish
Estefani	Crowned	Spanish
Estefania	Crowned	Spanish
Estefany	Crowned	Spanish
Estela	Star	Spanish
Estelita	Star	Spanish
Estella	Star	Spanish
Ester	Star	Arabic
Esteva	Crowned with laurels	Greek
Estrella	Star	Spanish

Estrellita	Star	Spanish
Eva	Life	Hebrew
Evita	Breath of life	Spanish
Exaltacion	Lifted up	Spanish
Ezmeralda	Emerald	Spanish
Faqueza	Weakness	Unknown
Fausta	Fortunate or lucky	Latin
Faustina	Fortunate or lucky	Latin
Fe	Trust or belief	Latin
Felicita	Fortunate or happy	Spanish
Felicitas	Fortunate or happy	Spanish
Felisa	Fortunate or happy	Spanish
Fermina	Strong	Spanish
Filipa	Lover of horses	Italian
Flor	Flower	Spanish
Florencia	Blooming or flowering	Spanish
Florentina	Blooming or flowering	Spanish
Florida	Blooming or flowering	Spanish
Florinia	Blooming or flowering	Latin
Florita	Blooming or flowering	Spanish
Fonda	Inn	Spanish
Fortuna	Fortunate or lucky	Latin
Francisca	Free or from France	Spanish
Freira	Sister	Unknown
Frescura	Freshness	Unknown
Galena	Healer	Greek

Galenia	Healer	Greek
Garabina	Purification	Spanish
Garabine	Purification	Spanish
Garaitz	Victory	Spanish
Garbina	Purification	Spanish
Garbine	Purification	Spanish
Gaspara	Treasurer	Spanish
Gechina	Grace	Spanish
Generosa	Generous	Spanish
Gertrudes	Beloved warrior	Spanish
Gertrudis	Beloved warrior	Spanish
Gezana	Reference to the Incarnation	Spanish
Gezane	Reference to the Incarnation	Spanish
Ginebra	White as foam	Celtic
Ginessa	White as foam	Celtic
Gitana	Gypsy	Spanish
Godalupe	Reference to the Virgin Mary	Spanish
Gorane	Holy cross	Unknown
Gotzone	Angel	German
Gracia	Beauty of form	Spanish
Graciana	Beauty of form	Spanish
Gregoria	Vigilant watchman	Spanish
Guadalupe	Valley of the wolf	Spanish
Guillelmina	Resolute protector	Italian/Spanish

Guillermina	Resolute protector	Italian/Spanish
Gustava	Staff of the Goths	Scandinavian
Henriqua	Ruler of the enclosure	Spanish
Hermina	Messenger	Spanish
Hermosa	Beautiful	Spanish
Honor	Honor	Latin
Honoratas	Honor	Spanish
Honoria	Honor	Latin
Hortencia	Gardener	Spanish
Idoia	Reference to the Virgin Mary	Spanish
Idurre	Reference to the Virgin Mary	Spanish
Ignacia	Fiery or ardent	Spanish
Igone	Ascension	Unknown
Ikerne	Visitation	Unknown
Ileanna	Light	Greek
Iliana	Light	Greek
Iluminada	Illuminated	Spanish
Imelda	Powerful fighter	German
Immaculada	The Immaculate Conception	Spanish
Ines	Pure	Spanish
Inez	Pure	Spanish
Inoceneia	Harmless or innocent	Spanish
Inocenta	Harmless or innocent	Spanish
Iratze	Reference to the Virgin Mary	Spanish

Irene	Peace	Greek
Irune	Reference to the Holy Trinity	Unknown
Isabel	Consecrated to God	Spanish
Isabela	Consecrated to God	Spanish
Isabella	Consecrated to God	Italian
Isidora	Gift of Isis	Latin
Itsaso	Sea	Unknown
Itxaro	Hope	Unknown
Ivette	Young archer	French
Izar	Star	Unknown
Izarra	Star	Unknown
Izarre	Star	Unknown
Izazkun	Reference to the Virgin Mary	Unknown
Jacinta	Hyacinth or purple	Spanish
Jaione	Reference to the Nativity	Unknown
Jakinda	Hyacinth	Unknown
Jasone	Assumption	Unknown
Javiera	Owner of a new house	Spanish
Jesusa	Jehovah is salvation	Spanish
Jimena	Heard	Spanish
Joaquina	God shall establish	Spanish
Jordana	To flow down or descend	Hebrew
Josefa	God will add	Spanish
Josefina	God will add	Spanish
Josune	Named for	Spanish

	Jesus	
Jovana	Majestic	Latin
Jovanna	Majestic	Latin
Jovena	Majestic	Latin
Jovina	Majestic	Latin
Jovita	Jovial	Latin
Juana	God is gracious	Spanish
Juanetta	God is gracious	Spanish
Juanisha	God is gracious	Spanish
Juanita	God is gracious	Spanish
Julia	Downy bearded or youthful	Latin
Julieta	Downy bearded or youthful	Spanish
Julina	Downy bearded or youthful	Latin
Karmen	Song	Hebrew
Kasandra	Doom	Greek
Katia	Pure	Unknown
Kemena	Strong	Unknown
Kemina	Strong	Unknown
Kesara	Youthful	Latin
Kesare	Youthful	Latin
La Reina	Queen	Unknown
Lala	Well spoken	Spanish
Lali	Well spoken	Spanish
Lalia	Well spoken	Spanish
Lalla	Well spoken	Spanish
Landa	Reference to the Virgin Mary	Basque

Landrada	Counselor	Spanish
Lara	Cheerful	Greek
Lareina	Sorrowful	Latin
Larunda	Crowned with laurels	Unknown
Latoya	Victorious one	American
Laura	Crowned with laurels	Latin
Laurana	Laurel tree	Latin
Laurencia	Crowned with laurels	Spanish
Laurinda	Crowned with laurels	Spanish
Laurita	Crowned with laurels	Spanish
Lavina	Purified	Latin
Lavinia	Purified	Latin
Lea	Tired or weary	Hebrew
Leala	Faithful or loyal	French
Legarre	Reference to the Virgin Mary	Unknown
Leira	Reference to the Virgin Mary	Basque
Leonor	Light	Greek
Leonora	Light	Greek
Lera	Reference to the Virgin Mary	Russian
Leticia	Joyful happy or glad	Latin
Letitia	Joyful happy or glad	Latin
Levina	Flash of lightning	Latin

Leya	Loyalty	Spanish
Lia	Bringer of good news	Greek
Liana	To bind or twine around	French
Liliana	Lily	Latin
Linda	Tender beauty	Spanish
Lola	Sorrow of the Virgin Mary	Spanish
Loleta	Sorrowful	Spanish
Lolita	Sorrowful	Spanish
Lolitta	Sorrowful	Spanish
Lora	Crowned with laurels	Latin
Lorda	Shrine of the Virgin Mary	Spanish
Lore	Flower	Latin
Lorena	Crowned with laurels	English
Loretta	Crowned with laurels	English
Lourdes	Shrine of the Virgin Mary	Spanish
Louredes	Shrine of the Virgin Mary	Spanish
Lucena	Bringer of light	Spanish
Lucila	Bringer of light	Latin
Lucita	Bringer of light	Spanish
Lucrecia	Rich reward	Spanish
Luella	Famous warrior	German
Luisa	Famous warrior	Spanish
Luiza	Famous	Spanish

	warrior	
Lupe	Wolf	Spanish
Lupita	Reference to the Virgin Mary	Spanish
Lur	Earth	Unknown
Luvenia	Little beloved one	Latin
Luvina	Little beloved one	Latin
Luz	Light	Spanish
Madalena	From the high tower	Spanish
Madalynn	From the high tower	Greek
Madelynn	From the high tower	Greek
Madena	From the high tower	Greek
Madia	From the high tower	Greek
Madina	From the high tower	Greek
Madre	Mother	Spanish
Magdalen	From the high tower	Greek
Magdalena	From the high tower	Spanish
Magdalene	From the high tower	English
Maite	Dearly loved	Spanish
Maitea	Dearly loved	Spanish
Malia	Bitter or sea of bitterness	Spanish
Malita	Bitter	Spanish
Manda	Battle maid	Spanish
Manoela	God is with us	Hebrew
Manuela	God is with us	Spanish

Marcela	Warlike	Spanish
Margarita	Pearl	Spanish
Maria	Bitter or sea of bitterness	Hebrew
Maricel	Warlike	Latin
Maricela	Warlike	Latin
Maricelia	Warlike	Latin
Maricella	Warlike	Latin
Marietta	Bitter or sea of bitterness	French
Marina	Sea maiden	Latin
Mariquita	Bitter or sea of bitterness	Spanish
Marisa	Of the sea	Latin
Marisela	Warlike	Latin
Marisol	Sunny sea	Spanish
Marquilla	Bitter	Spanish
Marta	Bitter	Hebrew
Martina	Warlike	Latin
Maya	Industrious	Latin
Melisenda	Sweet	French
Melita	Abbreviation of Carmelita	Spanish
Melosa	Sweet	Spanish
Melosia	Sweet	Spanish
Mendi	Reference to the Virgin Mary	Basque
Mercedes	Mercy or merciful	Spanish
Miguela	Who is like God	Spanish
Milagritos	Miracle	Spanish
Milagros	Miracle	Spanish
Milagrosa	Miracle	Spanish
Miranda	Admirable	Latin
Mirari	Miracle	Spanish

Mireya	Miracle	Spanish
Modesta	Modest	Spanish
Modeste	Modest	Spanish
Molara	Reference to the Virgin Mary	Basque
Monica	Advisor	Latin
Mora	Berry	Spanish
Morisa	Dark	Latin
Morissa	Dark	Latin
Naiara	Reference to the Virgin Mary	Unknown
Nalda	Strong	Unknown
Nana	Favor	Unknown
Narcisa	Daffodil	Greek
Natalia	Born at Christmas	Latin
Natividad	Reference to the Nativity	Spanish
Neiva	Snow	Spanish
Nekana	Sorrows	Unknown
Nekane	Sorrows	Unknown
Nelia	Yellow	Spanish
Nelida	Shining light	Unknown
Nerea	Mine	Unknown
Neva	Snow	Spanish
Nevada	Snowy	Spanish
Nicanora	Victorious army	Unknown
Nieva	Snow	Spanish
Nieve	Snowy	Unknown
Nina	Grace	Hebrew
Nita	Grace	Hebrew
Noemi	Pleasantness	Hebrew
Odanda	Famous land	Unknown
Oihane	From the forest	Unknown

Olimpia	Olympian	Greek
Olinda	Defender of the land	Spanish
Oliveria	Affectionate	Latin
Olivia	Olive tree	Latin
Ora	Gold	Spanish
Orquidea	Orchid	Spanish
Orquidia	Orchid	Spanish
Osana	Health	Unknown
Osane	Health	Unknown
Pabla	Little	Unknown
Paciencia	Patience	Latin
Palba	Blond	Basque
Palmira	From the city of palms	Spanish
Paloma	Dove	Spanish
Paquita	Free	Latin
Pastora	Shepherdess	German
Patricia	Noble	Latin
Paula	Small	Latin
Paulita	Little	Latin
Paz	Peace	Spanish
Pedra	Rock	Spanish
Pepita	He shall add	Hebrew
Perfecta	Perfect	Spanish
Pia	Pious	Latin
Piedad	Piety	Spanish
Pilar	Column or pillar	Spanish
Placida	Tranquil	Spanish
Presentacion	Presentation	Spanish
Primavera	Springtime	Spanish
Prudencia	Prudent	Latin
Puebla	From the city	Spanish
Pura	Pure	Spanish
Pureza	Pure	Spanish
Purificacion	Purification	Spanish

Purisima	Pure	Spanish
Querida	Beloved	Spanish
Quinta	Born fifth	Latin
Raimunda	Wise defender	Spanish
Ramira	Judicious	Spanish
Ramona	Mighty protector	Spanish
Raquel	Innocence of a lamb	French
Rebeca	Bound	Hebrew
Regina	Queen	Latin
Reina	Queen	Latin
Remedios	Remedy	Spanish
Ria	River	Spanish
Rica	Rules the home	Spanish
Ricarda	Rich and powerful ruler	Spanish
Rio	River	Spanish
Rita	Pearl	Greek
Rocio	Dew drops	Spanish
Roderiga	Notable leader	Spanish
Roldana	Famous	Unknown
Romana	From Rome	Latin
Rosa	Rose	Latin
Rosalia	Combination of Rose and Lily	Spanish
Rosalind	Beautiful	Spanish
Rosalinda	Beautiful rose	Spanish
Rosalinde	Beautiful	Spanish
Rosamaria	Bitter	Spanish
Rosario	Beautiful	Spanish
Rosemarie	Bitter flower	English
Rosiyn	Beautiful	Spanish

Rufa	Red haired	Latin
Rufina	Red haired	Latin
Sabana	From the open plain	Latin
Sabina	Ancient tribe of Central Italy	Latin
Salbatora	Savior	Spanish
Salvadora	Savior	Spanish
Salvatora	Savior	Italian
Sancha	Holy	Spanish
Sancia	Holy	Spanish
Sara	Princess	Hebrew
Sarita	Princess	Hebrew
Saturnina	Gift of Saturn	Spanish
Savanna	From the open plain	Spanish
Savannah	From the open plain	Spanish
Segunda	Born second	Spanish
Seina	Innocent	Basque
Senalda	Sign	Spanish
Senona	Lively	Spanish
Serafina	To burn	Latin
Serena	Calm or peaceful	Latin
Shoshana	Lily	Hebrew
Simona	God is heard	Hebrew
Socorro	Help	Spanish
Sofia	Wisdom	Greek
Solana	Sunshine	Spanish
Soledad	Solitary or solitude	Spanish
Soledada	Solitary	Spanish
Suelita	Little lily	Spanish
Susana	Lily	Hebrew
Tabora	Plays a small drum	Arabic

Tanis	Fairy queen	Slavic
Telma	Will	Unknown
Teodora	Gift of God	Czech
Terceira	Born third	Unknown
Teresa	Harvester	Greek
Teresita	Harvester	Greek
Tierra	Earth	Unknown
Trella	Star	Spanish
Ula	Well spoken	Basque
Ursula	Little female bear	Latin
Ursulina	Little female bear	Latin
Usoa	Dove	Unknown
Valentina	Healthy or strong	Latin
Vanesa	Butterfly	Greek
Ventura	Good fortune	Unknown
Verdad	Truthful	Spanish
Veronica	One who brings victory or true image	Latin
Vicenta	Victor	Latin
Vina	From the vineyard	Unknown
Virginia	Pure	Latin
Vittoria	Victorious	Latin
Viviana	Full of life, lively or alive	Latin
Xalbadora	Savior	Unknown
Xalvadora	Savior	Unknown
Xaviera	Owner of a new home	Basque
Xevera	Owns a new house	Basque
Xeveria	Owns a new house	Basque
Yadra	Mother	Unknown

Yanamaria	Bitter grace	Slavic
Yanamarie	Bitter grace	Slavic
Yesenia	Flower	Arabic
Yoana	God's gift	Hebrew
Yolanda	Violet	French
Zamora	Praised	Unknown
Zandra	Defender of mankind	Greek
Zaneta	God's gift	Spanish
Zanetta	God's gift	Spanish
Zanita	God's gift	Spanish
Zita	Little rose	Spanish
Zurina	White	Basque
Zurine	White	Basque
BOYS	**MEANING**	**ORIGIN**
Abrahan	Father of a multitude	Hebrew
Abran	Exalted father	Hebrew
Adan	Of the red earth	Unknown
Adriano	Dark	Latin
Agustin	Majestic	Latin
Alano	Handsome	Spanish
Alanzo	Noble and eager	Spanish
Alarico	Rules all	Spanish
Alba	Town on the white hill	Latin
Alberto	Bright nobility	Italian
Alejandro	Defender of mankind	Spanish
Alfonso	Noble and eager	Italian
Alfredo	Wise councelor	Spanish
Alonso	Eager for battle	Spanish
Alonzo	Eager for	Spanish

	battle	
Aluino	Noble friend	Unknown
Alvar	Army of elves	English
Alvaro	Elf army	Spanish
Alvino	White	Latin
Amadeo	Loves God	Latin
Amado	To love God	Latin
Ambrosio	Divine	Spanish
Amoldo	Power of an eagle	Spanish
Anastasio	Resurrection	Spanish
Andreo	Manly	Greek
Andres	Manly	Greek
Angel	Messenger	Latin
Angelino	Messenger	Latin
Angelo	Messenger	Latin
Anibal	Grace of God	Greek
Anselmo	Divine protection	Spanish
Anton	Priceless, inestimable or praiseworthy	Latin
Antonio	Priceless, inestimable or praiseworthy	Italian
Aquilino	Eagle	Latin
Archibaldo	Bold	Spanish
Arlo	The barberry	Spanish
Armando	Soldier	Spanish
Arturo	Noble	Italian
Aurelia	Gold	Latin
Aureliano	Golden	Spanish
Aurelio	Golden	Italian
Aurelius	Golden	Latin
Bartoli	Ploughman	Spanish
Bartolo	Ploughman	Italian

Bartolome	Ploughman	Spanish
Basilio	Kingly	Italian
Beinvenido	Welcome	Spanish
Beltran	Bright raven	Unknown
Bemabe	Son of comfort	Unknown
Bembe	Prophet	Unknown
Benedicto	Blessed	Spanish
Benjamin	Born of the right hand	Hebrew
Bernardo	Brave as a bear	Spanish
Berto	Distinguished	Spanish
Blanco	Blond	Spanish
Blas	Stammerer	Spanish
Bonifacio	To do good	Italian
Bonifaco	Benefactor	Latin
Buinton	Born fifth	Unknown
Calvino	Bald	Latin
Camilo	Ceremonial attendant	Latin
Carlomagno	Charlemagne	Spanish
Carlos	Manly	Spanish
Casimiro	Great destroyer	Polish
Cedro	Strong gift	Unknown
Cesar	Hairy	Latin
Cesario	Hairy	Latin
Cesaro	Hairy	Latin
Charro	Cowboy	Spanish
Che	God will add or multiply	Spanish
Chico	Boy	Spanish
Ciceron	Chickpea	Latin
Cidro	Strong gift	Spanish
Cipriano	From Cyprus	Spanish
Cirilo	Christ like	Greek

Ciro	Sun	Greek
Cisco	Free	Spanish
Claudio	Lame	Italian
Clemente	Merciful	Spanish
Clodoveo	Famous warrior	Unknown
Conrado	Honest or brave advisor	Spanish
Constantino	Constant or steadfast	Italian
Cornelio	Ivory colored	Spanish
Cortez	Conqueror	Spanish
Cris	Follower of Christ or anointed	Greek
Cristian	Follower of Christ or anointed	Greek
Cristiano	Follower of Christ or anointed	Spanish
Cristobal	Follower of Christ or anointed	Spanish
Cristofer	Follower of Christ or anointed	Greek
Cristofor	Follower of Christ or anointed	Italian
Criston	Follower of Christ or anointed	Greek
Cristos	Follower of Christ or anointed	Spanish
Cristoval	Follower of Christ or anointed	Spanish

Cruz	Cross	Spanish
Cuartio	Born fourth	Unknown
Cuarto	Born fourth	Unknown
Curcio	Polite or courteous	Spanish
Currito	Polite or courteous	Spanish
Curro	Polite or courteous	Spanish
Dacio	From Dacia	Spanish
Damario	Gentle	Spanish
Damian	To tame	Greek
Daniel	God is my judge	Hebrew
Danilo	God is my judge	Spanish
Dantae	Enduring	Latin
Dante	Enduring	Latin
Dantel	Enduring	Latin
Dario	Affluent or wealthy	Spanish
Daunte	Enduring	Latin
David	Beloved	Hebrew
Delmar	Of the sea	Latin
Demario	Gentle	Italian
Desiderio	Desired or longed for	Spanish
Diego	Supplanter	Spanish
Domenico	Belonging to the Lord	Italian
Domingo	Born on Sunday	Spanish
Donatello	Gift of God	Italian
Donato	Gift of God	Italian
Donzel	Gift of God	Unknown
Duardo	Prosperous guardian	Spanish
Duarte	Prosperous	Portuguese

	guardian	
Edgardo	Lucky spearman	Italian
Edmundo	Prosperous protector	Spanish
Eduardo	Wealthy guardian	Spanish
Edwardo	Wealthy guardian	Spanish
Efrain	Doubly fruitful	Hebrew
Elia	The Lord is my God	Hebrew
Elias	Jehovah is God	Hebrew
Eliazar	God has helped	Hebrew
Elija	The Lord is my God	Yiddish
Eloy	Chosen one	Latin
Elvio	Elfin	Spanish
Emanuel	God is with us	Hebrew
Emilio	Industrious	Spanish
Eneas	Praised	Greek
Enrique	Ruler of the estate	Spanish
Enzo	Ruler of the estate	German
Erasmo	Lovable	Spanish
Ernesto	Sincere	Spanish
Eron	Lofty or inspired	Unknown
Esequiel	God strengthens	Spanish
Esteban	Crowned	Spanish
Estefan	Crowned	Spanish
Estevan	Crowned	Spanish
Estevon	Crowned	Spanish
Eugenio	Well born or	Spanish

	noble	
Evarado	Hardy	Unknown
Everardo	Strong as a wild boar	Spanish
Ezequiel	Strength of God	Spanish
Fabio	Bean grower	Italian
Fanuco	Free	Unknown
Faron	Pharoah	Unknown
Farruco	Free	Spanish
Fausto	Fortunate or lucky	Italian
Federico	Peaceful ruler	Spanish
Feliciano	Fortunate or happy	Spanish
Felipe	Lover of horses	Spanish
Felippe	Lover of horses	Spanish
Felix	Fortunate or happy	Latin
Fermin	Strong	Spanish
Fernando	Adventurous and risky	Spanish
Fidel	Faithful	Latin
Fidele	Faithful	Latin
Flavio	Blond or fair haired	Italian
Florentino	Blooming or flowering	Spanish
Florinio	Blooming or flowering	Spanish
Fraco	Weak	Unknown
Francisco	Free or from France	Spanish
Franco	Free or form France	Spanish
Frasco	Free or from France	Spanish

Frascuelo	Free or from France	Spanish
Frederico	Peaceful ruler	Spanish
Fresco	Fresh	Unknown
Frisco	Free	Spanish
Gabino	God is my strength	Spanish
Gabriel	God is my strength	Hebrew
Gabrio	God is my strength	Spanish
Galeno	Healer	Spanish
Galtero	Strong warrior	Unknown
Garcia	Mighty with a spear	Spanish
Gaspar	Treasurer	French
Gaspard	Treasurer	French
Gasper	Treasurer	French
Generos	Generous	Spanish
Geraldo	Mighty with a spear	Spanish
Gerardo	Brave with a spear	Spanish
German	From Germany	German
Geronimo	Sacred	Italian
Gervasio	Honorable	Spanish
Gervaso	Honorable	Spanish
Gil	Illustrious pledge	Spanish
Gilberto	Illustrious pledge	Spanish
Gillermo	Resolute protector	Spanish
Godfredo	Friend of God	Spanish
Godofredo	God'd peace	Spanish
Gregorio	Vigilant watchman	Italian

Gualterio	Strong and powerful warrior	Italian
Guido	Life	Italian
Guillermo	Resolute protector	Spanish
Gustavo	Staff of the Goths	Italian/Spanish
Gutierre	Powerful ruler	Spanish
Hector	Steadfast	Greek
Heriberto	Illusrious warrior	Spanish
Hernan	Adventurous	Spanish
Hernandez	Adventurous	Spanish
Hernando	Adventurous	Spanish
Hilario	Cheerful or merry	Spanish
Honorato	Honor	Spanish
Horacio	Timekeeper	Spanish
Horado	Timekeeper	Spanish
Huberto	Bright mind	Spanish
Hugo	Bright mind	Latin
Humberto	Brilliant strength	Portuguese
Iago	Supplanter	Spanish
Ignacio	Fiery or ardent	Spanish
Ignado	Fiery or ardent	Spanish
Ignazio	Fiery or ardent	Italian
Incendio	Fire	Unknown
Inocencio	Harmless or innocent	Spanish
Inocente	Harmless or innocent	Spanish
Isadoro	Gift of Isis	Spanish

Isaias	God is my salvation	Spanish
Ishmael	God listens	Hebrew
Isidoro	Gift of Isis	Italian
Isidro	Gift of Isis	Spanish
Ismael	God listens	Arabic
Ivan	God is gracious	Russian
Jacinto	Hyacinth	Spanish
Jacobo	Supplanter	Spanish
Jago	Supplanter	English
Jaime	Supplanter	Hebrew
Jairo	God enlightens	Spanish
Javier	Owner of a new house	Spanish
Javiero	Born in January	Spanish
Jax	Alas	Unknown
Jeraldo	Mighty with a spear	Spanish
Jerardo	Mighty with aspear	Spanish
Jeremias	God will uplift	German
Jerico	City of the moon	Arabic
Jerold	Rules by the spear	English
Jeronimo	Holy name	Latin
Jerrald	Rules by the spear	English
Jerrold	Rules by the spear	English
Jesus	Jehovah is salvation	Hebrew
Joachim	God shall establish	Hebrew
Joaquin	God shall establish	Spanish

160

Jonas	Dove	Hebrew
Jorge	Farmer	Greek
Jose	God will add	Spanish
Joselito	God will add	Spanish
Josias	Jehovah has healed	Hebrew
Josue	God is salvation	French
Juan	God is gracious	Spanish
Juanito	God is gracious	Spanish
Julian	Downy bearded or youthful	Latin
Juliano	Downy bearded or youthful	Latin
Julio	Downy bearded or youthful	Spanish
Justino	Just	Spanish
Kemen	Strong	Basque
Lazaro	God will help	Italian
Leandro	Lion man or brave as a lion	Spanish
Leon	Brave as a lion	German
Leonardo	Brave as a lion	Italian/Spanish
Leonel	Young lion	English
Leonides	Brave as a lion	Russian
Leopoldo	Brave people	German
Lisandro	Liberator	Spanish
Lonzo	Ready for battle	Spanish
Lorenzo	Crowned with	Italian

	laurels	
Lucas	Bringer of light	Latin
Lucero	Bringer of light	Spanish
Luciano	Bringer of light	Italian
Lucila	Bringer of light	Latin
Lucio	Bringer of light	Spanish
Luis	Famous warrior	Spanish
Macario	Blessed	Spanish
Macerio	Blessed	Spanish
Mannie	God is with us	Spanish
Manny	God is with us	Spanish
Mano	God is with us	Spanish
Manolito	God is with us	Spanish
Manolo	God is with us	Spanish
Manuel	God is with us	Hebrew
Manuelo	God is with us	Spanish
Marco	Warlike	Italian
Marcos	Warlike	Spanish
Mariano	Bitter or sea of bitterness	Italian
Mario	Of the sea or sailor	Italian
Marquez	Nobleman	Portuguese
Martin	Warlike	Latin
Martinez	Warlike	Spanish
Martino	Warlike	Italian
Mateo	Gift of God	Spanish
Matias	Gift of God	Spanish
Matro	Gift from God	Unknown
Maureo	Dark skinned	Spanish
Mauricio	Dark skinned	Spanish
Mauro	Moorish	Spanish

Miguel	Who is like God	Spanish
Moises	Saved from the water	Hebrew
Montae	Mountain	Spanish
Montay	Mountain	Spanish
Monte	Mountain	Spanish
Montel	Mountain	Spanish
Montes	Mountain	Spanish
Montez	Mountain	Spanish
Montrel	Mountain	French
Montrell	Mountain	French
Montrelle	Mountain	French
Naldo	Strong	Spanish
Natal	Birth	Spanish
Natalio	Born at Christmas	Spanish
Natanael	Gift from God	Hebrew
Nataniel	Gift from God	Hebrew
Navarro	Plains	Spanish
Nemesio	Justice	Latin
Neron	Strong	Latin
Nesto	Serious	Spanish
Nestor	Traveler	Greek
Neto	Serious	Spanish
Nevada	Snowy	Spanish
Nicanor	Victorious army	Unknown
Nicolas	Victory of the people	Greek
Niguel	Champion	Unknown
Noe	Rest or comfort	French
Norberto	Brilliant hero	Scandinavian
Normando	Man of the north	French
Oliverio	Affectionate	Latin
Oliverios	Affectionate	Latin

Orlan	Renowned in the land	German
Orland	Renowned in the land	German
Orlando	Renowned in the land	German
Orlin	Renowned in the land	German
Orlondo	Renowned in the land	Spanish
Oro	Gold	Spanish
Pablo	Little or small	Spanish
Pacho	Free	Spanish
Paco	Free	Spanish
Pacorro	Free	Spanish
Palban	Blond	Basque
Palben	Blond	Basque
Pancho	Free	Spanish
Pascual	Passover	Italian
Pasqual	Passover	Italian
Patricio	Noble	Spanish
Patrido	Noble	Latin
Paulo	Small	Latin
Paz	Peace	Spanish
Pedro	Rock	Spanish
Pepe	He shall add	Italian
Pepillo	He shall add	Unknown
Pirro	Flaming hair	Greek
Platon	Broad shouldered	Greek
Ponce	Fifth	Spanish
Porfirio	Purple stone	Greek
Porfiro	Purple stone	Greek
Primeiro	Born first	Italian
Prospero	Fortunate or lucky	Latin
Pueblo	From the city	Spanish
Rafael	God has	Hebrew

	healed	
Rafe	God has healed	English
Rai	Mighty protector	Spanish
Raimundo	Mighty protector	Spanish
Ramirez	Judicious	Spanish
Ramiro	Judicious	Spanish
Ramon	Wisely	Spanish
Ramone	Wisely	Scandinavian
Raul	Wise counsel	French
Raulo	Wise	Lithuanian
Rayman	Wisely	English
Raymon	Wisely	English
Renaldo	Counselor ruler	Spanish
Renato	To rise again	Italian
Reno	Gambler	American
Rey	Kingly	Spanish
Reyes	Kingly	Spanish
Reynaldo	King's advisor	Spanish
Reynardo	Strong counselor	Spanish
Ricardo	Rich and powerful ruler	Spanish
Richie	Variant of Richard	English
Rico	Rich and powerful ruler	Spanish
Rio	River	Spanish
Ritchie	Variant of Richard	English
Roberto	Bright with fame	Spanish
Rodas	Garden of	Greek

	roses	
Rodas	Garden of roses	Greek
Roderigo	Notable leader	Spanish
Rodolfo	Famous wolf	Spanish
Rodrigo	Famous ruler	Spanish
Rogelio	Famous warrior	Spanish
Rolando	Famous land	Spanish
Roldan	Famous	Unknown
Roman	Roman	Latin
Romano	From Rome	Latin
Romeo	Pilgrim to Rome	Italian
Ronaldo	Rules with counsel	Portuguese
Roque	Rock	Unknown
Rosario	Rosary	Portuguese
Ruben	A son	Hebrew
Rufio	Red haired	Latin
Rufo	Red haired	Latin
Sabino	A Sabine	Basque
Sal	Savior	Italian
Salbatore	Savior	Italian
Salomon	Peaceful ruler	Hebrew
Salvador	Savior	Spanish
Salvadore	Savior	Spanish
Salvatore	Savior	Italian
Salvino	Savior	Unknown
Samuel	Heard by God	Hebrew
Sancho	Holy or sacred	Latin
Sanson	Of the sun	Spanish
Santiago	Supplanter	Spanish
Santos	Saints	Spanish
Saturnin	Gift of Saturn	Spanish
Saul	Longed for	Hebrew

Sebastiano	Revered	Italian
Segundo	Second	Spanish
Sein	Innocent	Basque
Senon	Lively	Spanish
Serafin	To burn	Latin
Severo	Severe	Spanish
Silverio	Greek god of trees	Spanish
Silvino	Greek god of trees	Spanish
Stefano	Crowned or crown of laurels	Italian
Tabor	Plays a small drum	Arabic
Tadeo	Praise	Arabic
Tajo	Day	Spanish
Taurino	Bull like	Spanish
Tauro	Bull like	Spanish
Tavio	Eighth	Latin
Teo	God	Unknown
Teodor	Gift of God	Greek
Teodoro	Gift of God	Greek
Terciero	Born third	Unknown
Teyo	God	Unknown
Timo	One who honors God	Scandinavian
Timoteo	One who honors God	Spanish
Tito	Of the giants	Italian
Tobias	God is good	Hebrew
Tohias	God is good	Hebrew
Toli	Ploughman	Unknown
Tomas	Twin	German
Tonio	Highly praiseworthy	Portuguese
Toro	Bull like	Spanish
Tulio	Lively	Spanish

Turi	Bear	Spanish
Ulises	Wrathful	Latin
Urbano	City dweller or from the city	Italian
Valentin	Strong	Latin
Venturo	Food fortune	Spanish
Veto	Intelligent	Unknown
Vicente	Conqueror	Spanish
Victor	Conqueror	Latin
Victoriano	Conqueror	Latin
Victorino	Conqueror	Spanish
Victorio	Conqueror	Spanish
Victoro	Victor	Latin
Vidal	Life	Spanish
Videl	Life	Spanish
Vincente	Conqueror	Spanish
Virgilio	Strong	Spanish
Vito	Vital	Latin
Xabat	Savior	Basque
Xalbador	Savior	Unknown
Xalvador	Savior	Unknown
Xavier	Owner of a new home	Basque
Xever	Owns a new house	Basque
Yago	Supplanter	Spanish
Zacarias	Remembered by the lord	Spanish
Zenon	Harness	Greek

Mythological Names

Some of the strongest people that have ever lived have done so because they received inspiration from their name. Mythological names come from a rich history of literature, fables, and even religious texts. Each name has various spellings, especially those that are present in different parts of the world. Mythological names will give your child a name that isn't all that common but will invoke a sense of responsibility in them.

GIRLS	MEANING	ORIGIN
Acantha	Thorn, Pickle	Greek
Aditi	Boundless, Freedom, Security	Indian
Adrasteia	Greek Goddess	Greek
Aegle	Light, Radiance	Greek
Aella	Whirlwind	Greek
Agaue	Noble	Greek
Aglaia	Splendour	Greek
Agrona	Battle	Celtic
Aino	The only one	Finnish
Alcyone	Kingfisher	Latin
Alecto	Unceasing	Greek
Alexandra	Feminine form of Alexander	Multiple
Althea	Healing	Greek
Amalthea	To soothe	Greek
Amaterasu	Heaven	Far East
Ameretat	Immortality	Persian
Anahita	Immaculate	Persian
Andraste	Invincible	Celtic
Angharad	More love	Welsh
Anthea	Flower	Greek
Aoife	Beautiful	Irish
Arachne	Spider	Greek
Arethusa	Quick, Nimble	Greek
Ariadne	Most Holy	Greek
Aretmis	Safe	Greek

Asherah	She who walks in the sea	Near Eastern
Ashtad	Justice	Persian
Ashtoreth	Goddess of Love	Biblical
Astraea	Star	Greek
Atalanta	Equal	Greek
Atropos	Inevitable, Inflexible	Greek
Aurora	Dawn	Latin
Bast	Fire	Egyptian
Bastet	Fire	Egyptian
Bebinn	Fair Lady	Irish
Bellona	To Fight	Roman
Bhumi	Earth	Hindu
Blathnat	Little Flower	Irish
Brahma	Prayer	Hindu
Bridget	Exalted One	Irish
Brunhild	Battle	German
Calliope	Music	Greek
Callisto	Musical	Greek
Calypso	She Who Conceals	Greek
Camilla	Fair Lady	Danish
Cardea	Axis	Roman
Carme	Shear	Greek
Cassandra	To Excel	Italian
Cassiopeai	Much Beauty	Greek
Ceres	To Grow	Roman
Chi	Spirital	African
Chloe	Green	Greek
Cliodhna	Shapely	Irish
Clytemenestra	Noble	Greek
Concordia	Harmony	Roman
Cybele	Hair	Near Eastern
Cynthia	Woman	Greek
Dalia	Lucky	Baltic

Danae	Greek	Greek
Daphne	Laurel	Greek
Deirdre	Woman	Irish
Demeter	Earth Mother	Greek
Derdriu	Mistress	Irish
Devi	Goddess	Indian
Diana	Divine	Italian
Dido	Virgin	Roman
Dike	Justice	Greek
Dione	Of God	Greek
Durga	Unattainable	Indian
Eos	Goddess of the dawn	Greek
Erato	Lyric and love poetry	Greek
Eris	Discord	Greek
Europa	Unknown	Greek
Euterpe	Music	Greek
Evadne	Well-pleasing	Greek
Fortuna	Goddess of fortune	Roman
Freya	Goddess of fertility	Norse
Frigg	Goddess of marriage	Norse
Fulla	Handmaiden	Norse
Gaea	Earth	Greek
Galatea	Ivory colored	Greek
Gefjon	Goddess of virgins	Norse
Godiva	God's gift	Old English
Gudrun	Friend in war	Norse
Hebe	Goddess of youth	Greek
Hela	Goddess of the underworld	Norse
Hera	Protectress	Greek
Hermione	Messenger	Greek

Hero	Unknown	Greek
Hestia	Goddess of the home	Greek
Hippolyte	Freer of horses	Greek
Hydra	Unknown	Greek
Idun	Goddess of immortality	Norse
Io	Heifer	Greek
Iris	Goddess of the rainbow	Greek
Iseult	Beautiful	Celtic
Isis	Goddess of the underworld	Egyptian
Ismini	Unknown	Greek
Jocasta	Unknown	Greek
Juno	Goddess of marriage	Roman
Kali	Dark one	Sanskrit
Kalliope	Beautiful voice	Greek
Kynthia	Goddess of the hunt	Greek
Latona	Unknown	Roman
Leda	Lady	Greek
Leto	Unknown	Greek
Maia	May	Greek
Medea	Cunning or wise	Greek
Medusa	Three	Greek
Melpomene	Tragedy	Greek
Melusine	Guardian of the home	French
Minerva	Goddess of wisdom	Roman
Nemesis	Revenge	Greek
Niobe	Unknown	Greek
Omphale	Unknown	Greek
Ops	Goddess of the	Roman

	earth	
Pallas	Maiden	Greek
Pax	Peace	Roman
Penelope	Weaver	Greek
Persephone	Goddess of spring	Greek
Phaidra	Bright one	Greek
Phoebe	Bright	Greek
Pixie	Mischievious	English
Polyhymnia	Sacred song	Greek
Polyxena	Hospitality	Greek
Psyche	Soul	Greek
Pyrrha	Red	Greek
Rhea	Goddess of the earth	Greek
Selene	Goddess of the moon	Greek
Semele	Unknown	Greek/Roman
Terpsichore	Dancing	Greek
Thalia	Comedy and poetry	Greek
Themis	Goddess of justice	Greek
Tyche	Goddess of fortune	Greek
Uma	Flax	Sanskrit
Urania	Astronomy	Greek
Venus	Goddess of love and beauty	Roman
Vesta	Goddess of home	Roman
BOYS	**MEANING**	**ORIGIN**
Achilles	Pain, Achelous River	Greek
Achilleus	Greek God	Greek
Adad	Cognate of Hadad	Middle Eastern

Name	Meaning	Origin
Aditya	Belonging in Aditi	Indian
Adonis	Greek God; "Lord"	Greek
Adrastos	Does Not Run Away	Greek
Áed	Older form of Aodh	Irish
Aeneas	Praise	Roman
Agamemnon	Steadfast	Greek
Agni	Fire	Indian
Ahura Mazda	Lord of Wisdom	Persian
Ailill	Elf	Irish
Aiolos	Quick, Nimble	Greek
Alberich	Power	German
Alexander	Defender of mankind	Multiple
Alvis	All wise	Norse
Amon	The Hidden One	Egyptian
An	Heaven	Sumerian
Anil	Air	Indian
Anubis	Royal Child	Egyptian
Aonghus	Strength	Scottish
Arash	Bright, truthfullness	Persian
Argus	Glistening, Shining	Greek
Arjuna	White, Clear	Indian
Atlas	Enduring	Greek
Atum	Completion	Egyptian
Ba'al	Lord	Indian
Bacchus	To Shout	Greek
Bahman	Good Mind	Persian
Bahram	Victory	Persian
Baladeva	Strength	Indian
Balder	Prince	Norse

Baldr	Prince	Norse
Baltazar	Balthazar	Christian
Barlaam	Unknown	Egyptian
Batraz	Unknown	Ossetian
Bedivere	Beauty	Welsh
Bedwyr	Romance	Welse
Belenos	Brilliant	Celtic
Belenus	Bright, truthfullness	Celtic
Beli	Brilliant	Welsh
Belial	Worthless	Judaism
Beowulf	Bee Wolf	Anglo-Saxon
Bharata	Maintained	Indian
Bhaskara	Shining	Indian
Bhima	Formidable	Hindu
Bile	Hero	Irish
Bran	Raven	Irish
Branwen	Beautiful Raven	Welse
Brijesha	Ruler of Brij	Indian
Brontes	Thunderer	Greek
Byeloblog	White	Slavic
Cael	Slender	Irish
Cai	Key	Welsh
Castor	To Protect	Greek
Cephalus	Head	Greek
Cepheus	To Think	Greek
Cerberus	Spotted	Greek
Charon	Fierce Brightness	Greek
Chyses	Golden	Greek
Chukwu	Great	African
Cian	Ancient tribe of Central Italy	Irish
Conall	Strong Wolf	Irish
Conor	Dog Lover	Irish
Consus	Planted	Roman

Cronus	To Cut	Greek
Cupid	Desire	Roman
Daedalus	Cunning	Greek
Dagan	Dragon	Near Eastern
Dagda	Good Mind	Irish
Dagon	Grain	Near Eastern
Daire	Fruitful	Greek
Damon	To Tame	Greek
Dazhdog	Giving	Slavic
Deimos	Terror	Greek
Dilipa	Protector	Hindu
Dipaka	Exciting	Indian
Dismas	Sunset	Christian
Drupada	Firm	Indian
Dwyn	Love	Celtic
Dylan	Great	Welsh
Ea	House of Water	Near Eastern
Echo	Echo	Greek
Eros	God of love	Greek
Eurus	The east wind	Greek
Eurystheus	Unknown	Greek
Fafner	Unknown	Teutonic
Fenrir	Unknown	Norse
Frey	God of fertility	Norse
Ganymede	Beautiful	Greek
Garm	Watchman of Hades	Norse
Gemini	Twin	Roman
Geryon	Three	Greek
Gunnar	Battle warrior	Norse
Hades	God of the underworld	Greek
Hagen	Strong defense	Teutonic
Hector	Steadfast	Greek
Heimdall	Watchman of the bridge	Norse

Helios	Sun God	Greek
Hephaestus	God of the fire or the forge	Greek
Heracles	Divine glory	Greek
Hercules	Glorious gift	Greek
Hermes	Messenger	Greek
Hogni	Unknown	Norse
Horus	God of the sun	Egyptian
Hymen	God of marriage	Greek/Roman
Icarus	Unknown	Greek
Ixion	Unknown	Greek
Janus	Passageway	Roman
Jove	Sky father	Greek
Jupiter	Sky father	Roman
Lares	Protector of the home	Roman
Leander	Lion man or brave as a lion	Greek
Loki	Mischievious	Norse
Lugh	God of the sun	Celtic
Manannan	God of the sea	Celtic
Manes	God of the underworld	Roman
Manu	Giver of laws	Sanskrit
Mars	War	Roman
Meleager	Unknown	Greek
Meneleus	Unknown	Greek
Mercury	God of invention	Roman
Merlin	Sea hill	Celtic
Minos	Unknown	Greek
Morpheus	God of dreams or sleep	Greek
Naiads	God of water	Greek
Narcissus	Self love	Greek
Neptune	God of the sea	Roman

Nester	Departing	Greek
Odin	God of all	Norse
Odysseus	Unknown	Greek
Oedipus	Unknown	Greek
Orion	Unknown	Greek/Roman
Orpheus	Unknwon	Greek
Osiris	Judge of the dead	Egyptian
Pan	God of nature	Greek
Pandarus	Unknown	Greek/Roman
Paris	Lover	Greek/Roman
Pax	Peace	Roman
Pegasus	Poetry	Greek
Philemon	Affectionate	Greek
Phoenix	Bright or red	Greek
Pluto	God of the underworld	Greek
Polynices	Unknown	Greek/Roman
Poseidon	God of the sea	Greek
Proteus	God of the sea	Greek
Ra	God of all	Egyptian
Saturn	God of agriculture	Roman
Siefried	Victorious peace	Teutonic
Sigurd	Guardian of victory	Norse
Sirius	Dog star	Greek
Tantalus	Tantalize	Greek
Theseus	Unknown	Greek
Thor	Thunder	Norse
Thoth	God of wisdom	Egyptian
Tristan	Tumalt	Celtic
Triton	Unknown	Greek
Try	God of war	Norse
Ull	God of archery	Norse
Ulysses	Wrathful	Roman

Uranus	Heaven	Greek
Vulcan	God of the fire or the forge	Roman
Zephyrus	West wind	Greek
Zeus	God of all	Greek
Bala	Young	Hindu
Chandra	Moon	Indian
Ananta	Infinite	Indian

Floral Names

If your baby is as beautiful and special as a flower, they deserve a name that is the same. While floral names are typically found for women, there are also options for males. Floral names are usually easier to pronounce and spell, but aren't all that common. We might all know a Rose, Lily, or a Daisy, but fewer people know an Aster. Keep an open mind and you might just find something that you like! If it helps, looking up these images will make it easier!

GIRLS	MEANING	ORIGIN
Calla	Beautiful	Greek
Camillia	Evergreen	Italian
Cherry	Cherry red	French
Cocoa	Coconut	Spanish
Daisy	Eye of the day	Old English
Fern	Darling	German
Fleur	Flower	French
Ginger	Pure	Latin
Hazel	Hazelnut	Old English
Heather	Flower	Old English
Holly	To prick	Old English

Iris	Rainbow	Greek
Ivy	Climber	Old English
Jasmine	Fragrant flower	Arabic
Juniper	Shrub	Latin
Laurel	Laurel tree	Latin
Lilac	Light blue purple	Arabic
Lily	Lily	Latin
Magnolia	Flowering tree	Latin
Nacisse	Daffodil	Latin
Olive	Olive tree	Latin
Pansy	Thoughtful	French
Rose	Flower	Latin
Sachet	Perfumed	Latin
Sage	Wise	Latin
Sorrel	Reddish brown	French
Sugar	Sweet	Unknown
Violet	Bluish purple	Latin
Willow	Graceful or Slender	English
Zinnia	Flower	Latin
BOYS	**MEANING**	**ORIGIN**
Aster	Star	Greek
Berry	Fruitful	Old English
Heath	A heath or a moor	Old English
Jonquil	Flower	Latin
Pepper	Unknown	Greek
Saffron	Unknown	Old English
Sequoia	Redwood	American

Celebrity

Do you have a celebrity that changed your life or that you look up to? It might seem a little strange at first, but many people name their babies after a celebrity! Think about how the names George and Charlotte spiked in popularity after Will and Kate named their babies, or think about how more and more people now have the name Hermione thanks to the Harry Potter series! Celebrity names are fun and exciting – and if you really don't want to, you don't even have to tell anyone that you really named your child after them!

GIRLS	MEANING	ORIGIN
Angelina	Actress Angelina Jolie	English
Beyonce	Singer Beyonce Knowles	American
Carmen	Actress Carmen Electra	Latin
Charlize	Actress Charlize Theron	Unknown
Demi	Actress Demi Moore	French
Felicity	Actress Felicity Huffman	English
Gisele	Supermodel Gisele Bundchen	Unknown
Gwyneth	Actress Gwyneth Paltrow	Welsh
Heidi	Supermodel Heidi Klum	German
Madonna	Singer and Actress Madonna	Unknown
Mariah	Singer Mariah Carey	Hebrew
Mena	Actress Mena Suvari	Unknown
Oprah	Talk Show Host and Actress Oprah Winfrey	Hebrew
Picabo	Olympic Downhill Skier Picabo Street	Unknown

Reese	Actress Reese Witherspoon	Welsh
Salma	Actress Salma Hayek	Arabic
Sela	Actress Sela Ward	Hebrew
Uma	Actress Uma Thurman	Sanskrit
Whoopi	Actress and Talk Show Host Whoopi Goldberg	Unknown
Yoko	Wife of John Lennon, Yoko Ono	Japanese
BOYS	**MEANING**	**ORIGIN**
Apolo	Olympic Speedskier Apolo Ohno	Greek
Bing	Actor and Singer Bing Crosby	Unknown
Bode	American Skier Bode Miller	Unknown
Chevy	Actor and Comedian Chevy Chase	French
Conan	Talk Show Host Conan O'Brien	Irish
Darren	Actor Darren Criss	Irish
Edgerrin	NFL Football Player Edgerrin James	Unknown
Elvis	Singer and Actor Elvis Presley	Scandinavian
Ewan	Actor Ewan McGregor	Scottish
Grace	Actor Grace Kelly	Latin
Harrison	Actor Harrison Ford	Old English
Hines	NFL Football Player Hines Ward	Unknown

Hulk	Actor and Pro Wrestler Hulk Hogan	Unknown
Humphrey	Actor Humphrey Bogart	German
Joaquin	Actor Joaquin Phoenix	Spanish
Keanu	Actor Keanu Reeves	Unknown
Kelsey	Actor Kelsey Grammer	Scottish
Marlon	Actor Marlon Brando	French
Mira	Actress Mira Sorvino	Latin
Montel	Talk Show Host Montel Williams	Spanish
Orson	Movie Director and Actor Orson Welles	Latin
Ozzy	Singer Ozzy Osbourne	Unknown
Pierce	Actor Pierce Brosnan	English
Plaxico	NFL Football Player Plaxico Burress	Unknown
Quentin	Movie Director Quentin Tarantino	Latin
Red	Comedian Red Skelton	Old English
Regis	Talk Show Host Regis Philbin	Unknown
Ringo	Singer and Musician Ringo Starr	Unknown
River	Actor River Phoenix	French
Rock	Actor Rock Hudson	English
Ronde	NFL Football Player Ronde Barber	Unknown

Russell	Actor Russell Crowe	French
Seal	Singer Seal	Unknown
Sylvester	Actor and Director Sylvester Stallone	Latin
Tiki	NFL Football Player Tiki Barber	Unknown
Tobey	Actor Tobey Maguire	Hebrew
Vin	Actor Vin Diesel	Unknown
Wolfgang	Chef Wolfgang Puck	German

French

French baby names are more romantic and beautiful than a lot of other names. However, they also tend to be difficult to pronounce and spell correctly. French names also tend to have many vowels, so if that is something you are looking for, it is a good place to start. You'll notice that while these are French names, they have a lot of other origins as well, making them a good way to compromise on a name. Whether you want an Adele or an Adrien, you will definitely have a baby with the most graceful name around.

GIRLS	MEANING	ORIGIN
Abella	Breath	French
Aceline	Noble	French
Adalene	Noble	English
Adalicia	Noble	French
Adalie	Noble	German
Adaliz	Noble	French
Adalyn	Noble	English
Addie	Noble	English
Adela	Noble	German
Adelaide	Noble	German
Adele	Noble	English

Name	Meaning	Origin
Adelia	Noble	English
Adelina	Noble	English
Adeline	Noble	English
Adelisa	Noble	German
Adelise	Noble	German
Adelle	Noble	German
Adelynn	Noble	English
Adilene	Noble	English
Adorlee	Adored	Latin
Adreanna	Dark	Italian
Adriane	Dark	English
Adrianna	Dark	Italian
Adrianne	Dark	English
Adriene	Dark	Latin
Adrienne	Dark	Latin
Afrodille	Daffodil	French
Agathe	Honorable or good	Greek
Aida	Helpful	Latin
Aiglentina	Sweetbrier rose	French
Aiglentine	Sweetbrier rose	French
Aimee	Dearly loved	French
Alaine	Attractive	Irish
Alair	Cheerful	French
Albertina	Noble	French
Alexandrine	Defender of mankind	French
Alexis	Defender of mankind	Greek
Alhertine	Noble	Unknown
Alisanne	Truthful	French
Alita	Winged	Spanish
Alix	Defender of mankind	Greek
Alixandra	Defender of mankind	Greek

Allaire	Cheerful	French
Alleffra	Cheerful	French
Allete	Winged	French
Allison	Truthful	Old English
Allyson	Truthful	Old English
Alsatia	From Alsace	French
Alyson	Truthful	Old English
Alyssandra	Defender of mankind	Greek
Amabella	Lovable	Latin
Amabelle	Lovable	Latin
Amalie	Industrious	German
Amarante	Flower that never fades	French
Amata	Lovable or dearly loved	Latin
Ambra	Amber	French
Ambre	Amber	French
Amedee	Loves God	Unknown
Amelie	Hard working	French
Ami	Dearly loved	French
Amia	Beloved	French
Amie	Beloved	French
Amite	Friend	Latin
Amitee	Friend	Latin
Amity	Friendship	Latin
Amy	Beloved	Latin
Ancelin	Handmaiden	French
Ancelina	Handmaiden	French
Andrea	Manly	Greek
Andree	Strong	Greek
Ange	Angel	French
Angela	Messenger	Latin
Angeletta	Little angel	French
Angelette	Little angel	French
Angelika	Messenger	German
Angelina	Messenger of	English

	God	
Angeline	Messenger of God	English
Angelique	Messenger of God	French
Angilia	Angel	French
Anne	Gracious	Hebrew
Annette	Gracious	French
Antoinette	Beyond praise	French
Apollina	Manly	Unknown
Apolline	Manly	Unknown
Arcene	Silvery	French
Ariane	Holy	French
Ariele	Lion of God	Hebrew
Arielle	Lion of God	Hebrew
Arjean	Silvery	French
Arleta	Pledge	Old English
Arletta	Pledge	Old English
Arlette	Pledge	Old English
Auberta	Bright or noble	French
Aubina	Blond	French
Aubine	Blond	French
Aubree	Blond ruler	French
Aubrey	Blond ruler	French
Aubriana	Blond ruler	French
Aubrianne	Blond ruler	French
Aubrie	Blond ruler	French
Aubry	Blond ruler	French
Auda	Old or wealthy	French
Aude	Old or wealthy	French
Audra	Noble strength	Old English
Audree	Noble strength	Old English

Aurore	Dawn	Latin
Austina	Majestic	Latin
Austine	Majestic	Latin
Avelaine	Hazelnut	French
Aveline	Hazelnut	French
Avice	Warlike	Unknown
Azura	Sky blue	Arabic
Azure	Sky blue	Arabic
Azurine	Sky blue	Arabic
Babette	Stranger	French
Bailee	Law enforcer or bailiff	Old English
Bailey	Law enforcer or bailiff	Old English
Baylee	Law enforcer or bailiff	Old English
Bayley	Law enforcer or bailiff	Old English
Baylie	Law enforcer or bailiff	Old English
Bel	Beautiful	French
Belda	Beautiful	French
Belle	Beautiful	French
Berangaria	Name of a princess	French
Berdine	Glorious and famous maiden	German
Berenice	She will bring victory	Greek
Bernadea	Brave as a bear	German
Bernadette	Brave as a bear	French
Bernadina	Brave as a bear	Italian
Bernadine	Brave as a bear	German

Bernarda	Brave as a bear	German
Berneen	Brave as a bear	German
Bernelle	Brave as a bear	German
Bernetta	Brave as a bear	German
Bernette	Brave as a bear	German
Bernice	One who brings victory	Greek
Berniss	One who brings victory	Greek
Bernita	Strong as a bear	Spanish
Bernyce	One who brings victory	French
Berthe	Bright ruler	German
Bette	God is my oath	French
Bettine	God is my oath	French
Blanch	White	French
Blanche	White	French
Blanchefleur	White flower	French
Blondell	Fair haired or blonde	French
Blondelle	Fair haired or blonde	French
Blondene	Fair haired or blonde	French
Bonnie	Pretty	English
Bonny	Pretty	English
Bret	From Britain	Irish
Brett	From Britain	Irish
Bretta	From Britain	Irish
Brettany	From Britain	English

Brette	From Britain	Irish
Bridgett	Strength	Irish
Bridgette	Strength	Irish
Brigette	Strength	Irish
Brigitte	Strong	French
Brucie	Brushwood or thicket	French
Brunella	Brown or dark haired	French
Cadence	Rhythm	Latin
Cadencia	Rhythmic	Spanish
Calandre	Lark	Greek
Calantha	Beautiful flower	Greek
Calanthe	Beautiful flower	Greek
Camila	Young ceremonial attendant	Spanish
Camile	Young ceremonial attendant	French
Camilla	Young ceremonial attendant	Italian
Camillei	Young attendant	French
Cammi	Young attendant	French
Candide	Bright or glowing white	French
Capucina	Cape	French
Capucine	Cape	French
Caress	Beloved	French
Caressa	Beloved	French
Caresse	Beloved	French
Carina	Maiden	Greek

Carine	Maiden	Greek
Carlotta	Little and womanly	Italian
Carnation	Flesh colored	Latin
Carol	Song of joy	French
Carola	Song of joy	French
Carole	Song of joy	French
Carolina	Little and womanly	Italian
Caroline	Little and womanly	French
Carressa	Beloved	French
Cateline	Pure	Greek
Cecile	Dim sighted or blind	French
Cecille	Dim sighted or blind	French
Celesse	Heavenly	Latin
Celeste	Heavenly	Latin
Celestia	Heavenly	Latin
Celestiel	Heavenly	French
Celestine	Heavenly	French
Celestyna	Heavenly	Spanish
Celie	Blind	French
Celine	Blind	French
Cendrillon	Of the ashes	Unknown
Cerise	Cherry or cherry red	French
Chanel	Chanel	English
Chanell	Chanel	English
Chanelle	Chanel	French
Channelle	Chanel	French
Chantae	Song	French
Chantal	Song	French
Chantalle	Song	French
Chantay	Song	French
Chante	Song	French
Chantel	Song	French

Chantell	Song	French
Chantelle	Song	French
Chantrell	Song	French
Chardae	Manly	French
Charee	Darling	French
Charlaine	Little and womanly	English
Charlayne	Little and womanly	English
Charleen	Little and womanly	English
Charleena	Little and womanly	English
Charlena	Little and womanly	English
Charlene	Little and womanly	Old English
Charlette	Little and womanly	French
Charline	Little and womanly	English
Charlisa	Little and womanly	French
Charlita	Little and womanly	French
Charlotta	Little and womanly	French
Charlotte	Little and womanly	French
Charmain	Song	French
Charmaine	Song	French
Charmayne	Song	French
Charmine	Song	French
Chaunte	Song	French
Chauntel	Song	French
Chenelle	Chanel	English
Cher	Beloved	French
Chere	Beloved	French

Cheree	Beloved	French
Chereen	Beloved	French
Cherell	Beloved	French
Cherelle	Beloved	French
Cheri	Beloved	French
Cherie	Beloved	French
Cherina	Beloved	Unknown
Cherine	Beloved	Unknown
Cherise	Dear one or darling	French
Cherita	Beloved	Spanish
Cherree	Beloved	French
Cherrelle	Beloved	French
Cherry	Cherry red	French
Cheyanna	Tribal name	American
Cheyanne	Tribal name	American
Cheyenne	Tribal name	American
Chiana	Unknown	American
Chianna	Unknown	American
Christiane	Follower of Christ or anointed	French
Christine	Follower of Christ or anointed	Greek
Cinderella	Of the ashes	French
Clair	Bright or clear	French
Claire	Bright or clear	French
Clara	Bright or Clear	Latin
Clare	Bright or Clear	Latin
Clarette	Clear	French
Claribel	Bright and beautiful	Latin
Clarice	Bright or	Italian

193

Name	Meaning	Origin
	Clear	
Clarinda	Bright or clear	Spanish
Clarisse	Bright or Clear	Latin
Clarita	Bright or Clear	Spanish
Claudette	Lame	French
Claudine	Lame	French
Clemence	Merciful	Latin
Clementina	Merciful	Latin
Clementine	Merciful	Latin
Coco	Coconut	Spanish
Coletta	Victory of the people	French
Colette	Victory of the people	French
Colletta	Victory of the people	French
Collette	Victory of the people	French
Comfort	Rest	Latin
Comforte	Rest	Latin
Constance	Constant or steadfast	Latin
Constancia	Constant or steadfast	Spanish
Coralie	Maiden	American
Coretta	Maiden	Greek
Corette	Maiden	Greek
Corinne	Maiden	Greek
Cortney	Courtier or court attendant	English
Cosette	Victorious	French
Courtlyn	Courtly or courteous	English

Courtney	Courtier or court attendant	English
Creissant	To create	French
Crescent	To create	French
Daisi	Eye of the day	Old English
Damia	To tame	Greek
Damiana	To tame	Greek
Damiane	To tame	Greek
Damien	To tame	Greek
Darcel	Fortress	French
Darcell	Fortress	French
Darcelle	Fortress	French
Darcey	Fortress	French
Darchelle	Fortress	French
Darci	Dark	Irish
Darcia	Fortress	French
Darcie	Fortress	French
Darcy	Fortress	French
D'Arcy	Fortress	French
Daveney	Beloved	English
Delight	Pleasure	English
Delit	Gives pleasure	French
Delmare	Of the sea	French
Delphine	Dolphin	Greek
Denice	God of wine	English
Deniece	God of wine	French
Denise	God of wine	French
Denisha	God of wine	American
Denissa	God of wine	French
Denisse	God of wine	French
Dennise	God of wine	French
Denyse	God of wine	English
Desarae	Desired or longed for	French

Desaree	Desired or longed for	French
Desideria	Desired or longed for	French
Desirae	Desired or longed for	French
Desirat	Desired or longed for	French
Desire	Desired or longed for	English
Desiree	Desired or longed for	French
Destanee	Fate	French
Destine	Fate	French
Destinee	Fate	French
Destini	Fate	French
Destinie	Fate	French
Destiny	Fate	French
Devan	Poet	Irish
Devana	From Devonshire	English
Devanna	From Devonshire	English
Devin	Poet	Irish
Devona	From Devonshire	English
Devondra	From Devonshire	English
Devonna	From Devonshire	English
Devonne	From Devonshire	English
Devyn	Poet	Irish
Devynn	Poet	Irish
Dezirae	Desired or longed for	French
Deziree	Desired or longed for	french
Di	Divine	Latin

Diahann	Divine	Latin
Diahna	Divine	Latin
Diamanta	Of high value	Latin
Dian	Divine	Latin
Diana	Divine	Latin
Diandra	Manly	American
Diane	Divine	Latin
Dianna	Divine	Latin
Diannah	Divine	Latin
Dianne	Divine	Latin
Dior	Golden	French
Dixie	Tenth	French
Domenique	Belonging to the Lord	French
Dominique	Belonging to the Lord	French
D'or	Golden	French
Dore	Golden	French
Doreen	Golden	French
Dorene	Golden	French
Dorine	Golden	French
Dory	Golden	French
Dyana	Divine	Latin
Dyann	Divine	Latin
Dyanna	Divine	Latin
Edmee	Prosperous protector	French
Eglantina	Wild rose	Unknown
Eglantine	Wild rose	Unknown
Elaina	Light	French
Elaine	Light	French
Elayna	Light	French
Eleanor	Light	Greek
Eleonore	Light	French
Eleta	Chosen	Unknown
Eliane	God has answered me	Hebrew

Name	Meaning	Origin
Elicia	God is my oath	Hebrew
Elienor	Light	Greek
Elinore	Light	Greek
Elisa	God is my oath	Greek
Elisabeth	God is my oath	Hebrew
Elisamarie	God is my oath	French
Elise	God is my oath	French
Elisha	God is my salvation	Hebrew
Elishia	God is my oath	Hebrew
Elita	Chosen	Latin
Eliza	God is my oath	Hebrew
Ella	Foreign	French
Ellaine	Light	French
Ellayne	Light	French
Ellinor	Light	Greek
Eloisa	Famous in war	French
Eloise	Famous in war	French
Eloisee	Famous in war	French
Emeline	Flatterer	French
Emeraude	Emerald	French
Emmaline	Industrious	French
Emmalyn	Industrious	American
Emmeline	Industrious	French
Emmy	Industrious	German
Esme	Emerald	French
Esmeraude	Emerald	French
Esperanza	Hope	Spanish

Estee	Star	English
Estelle	Star	French
Eugenia	Well born or noble	French
Eugenie	Well born or noble	French
Eulalie	Well spoken	French
Evelyn	Life	Old English
Evon	Archer	French
Evonna	Archer	French
Evonne	Archer	French
Evony	Archer	French
Fabienne	Bean grower	French
Fae	Trust or belief	French
Fanchon	Free	French
Fanchone	Free	French
Fanetta	Free	French
Fanette	Free	French
Fantina	Childlike	Unknown
Fantine	Childlike	French
Faun	A young dear	French
Fauna	A young dear	French
Faunia	A young dear	French
Favor	Approval	Latin
Fawnia	A young deer	French
Fay	Fairy	French
Fayanna	Fairy	French
Faye	Fairy	French
Fayette	Little fairy	French
Fayme	Famed	French
Fealty	Faithful	French
Felecia	Fortunate or happy	Latin
Felicia	Fortunate or happy	Latin
Felicienne	Fortunate or happy	French

Name	Meaning	Origin
Felicity	Fortunate or happy	English
Fifi	God will add	French
Fifine	God will add	French
Filicia	Fortunate or happy	Latin
Fleur	Flower	French
Fleurette	Little flower	French
Floressa	Blooming or flowering	French
Floretta	Blooming or flowering	French
Flori	Flower	Basque
Floria	Flower	Basque
Floriana	Blooming or flowering	Latin
Florida	Blooming or flowering	Spanish
Florinda	Blooming or flowering	Spanish
Florrie	Flower	English
Fontanne	Fountain	French
France	Free	Latin
Francena	Free or from France	French
Francene	Free or from France	French
Francille	Free or from France	French
Francina	Free or from France	French
Francine	Free or from France	French
Francoise	Free or from France	French
Gabrielle	God is my strength	French
Gaetana	From Gaete	Italian
Gaetane	From Gaete	Italian

Gala	Enjoyment	Norwegian
Galatee	White	French
Galla	Singer	Scandinavian
Gallia	Singer	Scandinavian
Garland	Crowned with flowers	French
Garnet	Pomegranate seed	English
Gay	Light hearted	French
Gemma	Precious stone	Latin
Geneva	Juniper	French
Geneve	Juniper	French
Genevie	White wave	French
Genevieve	White wave	French
Genevre	Juniper	Welsh
Genivee	White wave	French
Georgette	Farmer	French
Georgine	Farmer	English
Georgitte	Farmer	French
Germain	From Germany	French
Germaine	From Germany	French
Germana	From Germany	French
Gisella	Pledge	Italian/Spanish
Giselle	Pledge	German
Halette	Little Hal	French
Hanrietta	Ruler of the household	French
Hanriette	Ruler of the household	French
Harriet	Ruler of an enclosure	French
Harriett	Ruler of an enclosure	French
Harrietta	Ruler of the	French

	enclosure	
Harriette	Ruler of an enclosure	French
Hedvige	Battle maiden	Scandinavian
Helaine	Light	French
Helene	Light	French
Heloise	Famous warrior	French
Henrietta	Ruler of the enclosure	English
Henriette	Ruler of the enclosure	French
Hettie	Ruler of the enclosure	English
Hilaire	Cheerful or merry	French
Holly	To prick	Old English
Honore	Honor	French
Huette	Bright mind	French
Hugette	Bright mind	French
Huguetta	Bright mind	French
Ila	Light	Hungarian
Isabeau	Consecrated to God	French
Iva	God is gracious	Slavic
Ivonne	Young archer	French
Jacalyn	Supplanter	American
Jacinthe	Hyacinth	Spanish
Jacqualine	Supplanter	French
Jacqueleen	Supplanter	French
Jacqueline	Supplanter	French
Jacquelyn	Supplanter	French
Jacquelyne	Supplanter	French
Jacquelynne	Supplanter	French
Jacquenetta	Little supplanter	French

Jacquenette	Little supplanter	French
Jaquelin	Supplanter	French
Jasmeen	Fragrant flower	Arabic
Jasmin	Fragrant flower	Arabic
Jasmyne	Fragrant flower	Arabic
Jazmine	Fragrant flower	Arabic
Jazzmine	Fragrant flower	Arabic
Jazzmyn	Fragrant flower	Arabic
Jean	God is gracious	French
Jeana	God is gracious	French
Jeane	God is gracious	French
Jeanee	God is gracious	French
Jeanetta	God is gracious	French
Jeanette	God is gracious	French
Jeanice	God is gracious	French
Jeanie	God is gracious	French
Jeanina	God is gracious	French
Jeanine	God is gracious	French
Jeanna	God is gracious	French
Jeanne	God is gracious	French

Name	Meaning	Origin
Jeannette	God is gracious	French
Jeannie	God is gracious	French
Jeannine	God is gracious	French
Jeena	God is gracious	French
Jehane	God is gracious	French
Jenette	God is gracious	French
Jenina	God is gracious	French
Jenine	God is gracious	French
Jennine	God is gracious	French
Jessamina	Fragrant flower	Arabic
Jessamine	Fragrant flower	Arabic
Jessamyn	Fragrant flower	Arabic
Jewel	Rare excellence	Latin
Jineen	God is gracious	Unknown
Joanna	God is gracious	English
Joanne	God is gracious	English
Jocelina	Joyous	Spanish
Joceline	Joyous	Latin
Jocelyn	Joyous	Latin
Jocelyne	Joyous	Latin
Jocelynn	Joyous	Latin
Joeliyn	God is willing	Hebrew
Joell	God is willing	Hebrew

Joella	God is willing	Hebrew
Joelle	God is willing	Hebrew
Joellen	God is willing	Hebrew
Joi	Rejoicing	French
Joia	Rejoicing	French
Joie	Rejoicing	French
Jolee	Pretty	French
Joleigh	Pretty	French
Joli	Pretty	French
Jolie	Pretty	French
Jordane	To flow down to descend	Hebrew
Josalyn	Joyous	Latin
Josalynn	Joyous	Latin
Joscelyn	Joyous	Latin
Josepha	God will add	German
Josephe	God will add	Italian
Josephina	God will add	Spanish
Josephine	God will add	French
Josette	God will add	French
Josilyn	Joyous	Latin
Joslin	Joyous	Latin
Joslyn	Joyous	Latin
Joy	Rejoicing	Latin
Joya	Rejoicing	Latin
Joyann	Rejoicing	English
Joyanna	Rejoicing	English
Joyanne	Rejoicing	English
Joyelle	Rejoicing	French
Jozlyn	Joyous	American
Jule	Jewel	English
Julee	Downy bearded or youthful	English
Juleen	Downy bearded or youthful	Basque

205

Julia	Downy bearded or youthful	Latin
Julie	Downy bearded or youthful	English
Julienne	Downy bearded or youthful	French
Juliet	Downy bearded or youthful	French
Julietta	Downy bearded or youthful	Italian
Juliette	Downy bearded or youthful	French
Julita	Downy bearded or youthful	Spanish
Justeen	Just	Latin
Justyne	Just	Latin
Kamille	Free born or noble	French
Karcsi	Joyful song	Unknown
Kari	Pure	Greek
Karla	Farmer	German
Karlotta	Tiny and feminine	Spanish
Karolina	Tiny and feminine	Slavic
Karoline	Tiny and feminine	German
Karoly	Strong and manly	Slavic
Katriane	Pure	French
La Row	Red haired	French
La Vergne	Born in the	French

	spring	
La Verne	Born in the spring	French
Lace	Cheerful	Latin
Lacee	Cheerful	Latin
Lacene	Cheerful	French
Lacey	Cheerful	Latin
Laci	Cheerful	Latin
Laciann	Cheerful	Latin
Lacie	Cheerful	Latin
Lacina	Cheerful	Spanish
Lacy	Cheerful	Latin
Lacyann	Cheerful	English
Laurel	Laurel tree	Latin
Lauren	Crowned with laurels	English
Laurene	Crowned with laurels	English
Laurette	Little laurel	French
Lavern	Woodland or grove of alder trees	French
Laverna	Woodland or grove of alder trees	French
Laverne	Woodland or grove of alder trees	French
Lavernia	Woodland or grove of alder trees	French
Laycie	Cheerful	Latin
Leala	Faithful or loyal	French
Lealia	Faithful or loyal	French
Lela	Faithful	French
Leola	Brave as a	German

	lioness	
Leona	Brave as a lioness	German
Leonarda	Brave as a lioness	German
Leonda	Lion or lioness	German
Leondra	Lion or lioness	German
Leondrea	Lion or lioness	German
Leone	Brave as a lion	Italian
Leonela	Young lioness	English
Leonelle	Young lioness	English
Leonie	Brave as a lion	French
Leonore	Light	Greek
Leontina	Like a lioness	Latin
Letje	Tiny and womanly	Unknown
Letya	Tiny and womanly	Unknown
Liana	To bind or twine around	French
Liane	To bind or twine around	French
Liealia	Loyal	Unknown
Lili	Lily	Latin
Liliane	Lily	Latin
Linette	Bird	French
Liriene	Reads aloud	French
Lirienne	Reads aloud	French
Lise	Consecrated to God	German
Lissette	Consecrated to God	French
Logestilla	Legend	Unknown

Logistilla	Legend	Unknown
Loraina	From Lorraine	French
Loraine	From Lorraine	French
Lorayne	From Lorraine	French
Lorin	Crowned with laurels	American
Lorraina	From Lorraine	French
Lorraine	From Lorraine	French
Lotye	Tiny and womanly	German
Louella	Famous warrior	German
Louisa	Famous warrior	English
Louise	Famous warrior	German
Lucette	Bringer of light	French
Lucie	Bringer of light	French
Lucienne	Bringer of light	French
Lucile	Bringer of light	French
Lucille	Bringer of light	French
Lucrece	A Roman matron	French
Lundy	Monday	French
Lynnette	Waterfall	French
Lyonette	Little lion	French
Lyra	Expression of emotion	Greek
Lyric	Expression of	Greek

	emotion	
Mabelle	Lovable	Latin
Macee	Weapon	French
Macey	Weapon	French
Macy	Weapon	French
Madalene	From the high tower	Greek
Maddy	From the high tower	English
Madeleina	From the high tower	French
Madeleine	From the high tower	French
Madelina	From the high tower	Italian
Madeline	From the high tower	Greek
Madelon	From the high tower	French
Madie	From the high tower	English
Madolen	From the high tower	Greek
Mae	Great	English
Maelee	Great	Latin
Maelynn	Great	Latin
Magnolia	Flowering tree	Latin
Mai	May	French
Maia	May	Greek
Maiolaine	Flower	French
Maiya	May	French
Majori	Pearl	Greek
Mallory	Unfortunate or unlucky	French
Manette	Bitter	French
Manon	Bitter	French
Marcella	Warlike	Latin

Marcelle	Warlike	French
Marcellia	Warlike	Latin
Marchelle	Warlike	American
Maree	Bitter or sea of bitterness	French
Margaux	Pearl	French
Margeaux	Pearl	French
Margery	Pearl	Unknown
Margo	Pearl	French
Margot	Pearl	French
Marguerite	Pearl	French
Maria	Bitter or sea of bitterness	Hebrew
Mariah	Bitter or sea of bitterness	Hebrew
Marian	Bitter or sea of bitterness	English
Mariane	Bitter or sea of bitterness	English
Marianne	Bitter or sea of bitterness	French
Marie	Bitter or sea of bitterness	French
Mariele	Bitter or sea of bitterness	Dutch
Marielle	Bitter or sea of bitterness	French
Marietta	Bitter or sea of bitterness	French
Mariette	Bitter or sea of bitterness	French
Marjolaina	Flower	Spanish
Marquisa	Noblewoman	French
Marquise	Noblewoman	French
Marquisha	Royalty	Unknown
Marteena	Warlike	Latin
Marveille	Miracle	French

Marvel	Miracle	French
Marvella	Miracle	French
Marvelle	Miracle	French
Maryl	Blackbird	Unknown
Mathilda	Mighty battle maiden	German
Mathilde	Mighty battle maiden	German
Matilda	Mighty battle maiden	German
Matilde	Mighty battle maiden	German
Mattie	Mighty battle maiden	English
Matty	Mighty battle maiden	English
Maud	Mighty battle maiden	English
Maude	Mighty battle maiden	English
Maura	Bitter	Irish
Maureen	Bitter	Irish
Maurelle	Dark and elfin	French
Maurina	Dark skinned	French
Maurine	Dark skinned	French
Mavis	Joy	French
Mavise	Joy	French
Melaina	Dark skinned	Greek
Melaine	Dark skinned	Greek
Melanee	Dark skinned	Greek
Melanie	Dark skinned	Greek
Melisande	Honey bee	French
Melodie	Melody or song	Greek
Melusina	Dark skinned	Spanish
Mercer	Merchant	English
Merci	Merciful	English

Mercy	Merciful	English
Merla	Blackbird	Latin
Merlyn	Blackbird	Latin
Merryl	Blackbird	Latin
Meryl	Blackbird	Latin
Michela	Who is like God	Hebrew
Michele	Who is like God	Hebrew
Michella	Who is like God	French
Michelle	Who is like God	French
Mignon	Delicate	French
Mignonette	Delicate	French
Millicent	Industrious	English
Millicente	Industrious	English
Millie	Industrious	English
Mimi	Resolute protector	French
Minetta	Resolute protector	French
Minette	Resolute protector	French
Minna	Resolute protector	German
Minnie	Resolute protector	American
Mirabella	Of incredible beauty	Latin
Mirabelle	Of incredible beauty	Latin
Mireille	Miracle	French
Mirla	Blackbird	Latin
Mistique	Air of mystery	French
Moniqua	Wise	French
Monique	Wise	French

Moreen	Dark skinned	French
Musetta	A song	French
Musette	A song	French
Mychele	Who is like God	French
Mychelle	Who is like God	French
Myrla	Blackbird	Latin
Mystique	Air of mystery	French
Nadeen	Hopeful	Russian
Nadine	Hopeful	Russian
Nan	Full of grace	English
Nancey	Full of grace	English
Nanci	Full of grace	English
Nancie	Full of grace	English
Nancy	Full of grace	English
Nanette	Full of grace	French
Nanine	Full of grace	French
Nann	Full of grace	French
Nannette	Full of grace	French
Nanon	Full of grace	French
Natalee	Born at Christmas	Latin
Natalie	Born at Christmas	French
Natalii	Born at Christmas	Russian
Nathalee	Birthday of Christ	Russian
Nathalia	Birthday of Christ	Russian
Nathalie	Birthday of Christ	Russian
Nathaly	Birthday of Christ	Russian
Natuche	Born at Christmas	French

Nichol	Victory of the people	French
Nichole	Victory of the people	French
Nicola	Victory of the people	Italian
Nicolette	Victory of the people	French
Ninette	Full of grace	French
Ninon	Full of grace	French
Noel	Christmas	French
Noele	Christmas	French
Noell	Christmas	French
Noella	Christmas	French
Noelle	Christmas	French
Noemie	Pleasantness	Hebrew
Nynette	Prayer	French
Odeletta	Little spring	French
Odelette	Little spring	French
Odette	Wealthy	French
Odila	Wealthy	French
Odile	Wealthy	French
Olympe	Heavenly	Greek
Olympia	Heavenly	Greek
Ophelia	Helper	Greek
Ophelie	Helper	Greek
Orane	Green	Irish
Oriel	Golden	Latin
Orlena	Gold	French
Orlene	Gold	French
Orlina	Gold	French
Orva	Worth gold	French
Page	Attendant	French
Paige	Attendant	French
Pansy	Thoughtful	French
Parnella	Rock	Unknown
Pascala	Born at	French

	Easter	
Pascale	Born at Easter	French
Pascaline	Born at Easter	French
Pasclina	Born at Easter	French
Patience	Enduring	Latin
Patrice	Noble	French
Pensee	Thoughtful	Unknown
Phillipa	Lover of horses	Greek
Pierretta	Rock	French
Pierrette	Rock	French
Prunella	Brown	Latin
Prunellie	Brown	Latin
Rachelle	Innocence of a lamb	Hebrew
Raina	Queen	Latin
Raison	Thinker	French
Raissa	Rose	Russian
Reina	Queen	Latin
Reine	Queen	Latin
Rene	Reborn	French
Renee	Reborn	French
Riva	From the shore	French
Rive	From the shore	French
Robinetta	Small robin	French
Robinette	Small robin	French
Roesia	Rose	French
Rohais	Rose	French
Roial	Regal	French
Romaine	From Rome	French
Romana	From Rome	Latin
Rosamonde	Famous guardian	German

Rose	Flower	Latin
Rosemaria	Bitter flower	English
Rosemarie	Bitter flower	English
Roux	Red	French
Roxane	Dawn of day	Greek
Roxanne	Dawn of day	Greek
Royale	Regal	English
Rubie	Reddish	Latin
Ruby	Reddish	Latin
Searlait	Tiny and womanly	French
Sibyla	Prophetess	Greek
Sidonia	Enticing	Hebrew
Sidonie	Follower of Saint Denys	French
Silana	Dignified	Unknown
Simone	Heard	Hebrew
Slainie	Health	Unknown
Slania	Health	Unknown
Slanie	Health	Unknown
Solaina	Dignified	French
Solaine	Dignified	French
Solange	Dignified	French
Stefania	Crowned or crown of laurels	French
Stephanie	A crown of garland	French
Susanne	Lily	English
Suzanne	Lily	English
Suzette	Little lily	French
Sydnee	Wide meadow	French
Sydney	Wide meadow	French
Tallis	Woodland	French
Tempeste	Stormy	French

Therese	Harvester	Greek
Tiffanie	Epiphany	French
Tiffney	Epiphany	French
Tilda	Mighty battle maiden	German
Tilly	Mighty battle maiden	German
Tracy	Warrior	Latin
Trinetta	Little innocent	Greek
Trinette	Little innocent	Greek
Vafara	To be strong	Unknown
Valeraine	To be strong	French
Valere	To be strong	French
Valerie	To be strong	Latin
Vedetta	Sentry	Italian
Vedette	Sentry	Italian
Veronique	One who brings victory or true image	French
Victorina	Victory	French
Victorine	Victory	French
Vignetta	Little vine	French
Vignette	Little vine	French
Villetta	Small town	French
Villette	Small town	French
Violetta	Little violet	French
Viollette	Little violet	French
Viviane	Full of life, lively or alive	French
Vivien	Full of life, lively or alive	French
Vivienne	Full of life, lively or alive	French
Voleta	Veiled	French
Voletta	Veiled	French

Xavierra	Owner of a new home	Basque
Xavierre	Owner of a new home	Basque
Ynes	Chaste	French
Ynez	Chaste	French
Yolanda	Violet	French
Yolande	Violet	French
Yolanthe	Strong	Unknown
Yolonda	Violet	French
Ysabel	Devoted to God	Spanish
Yseult	Fair	Irish
Yvette	Archer	French
Yvonna	Archer	French
Yvonne	Archer	French
Zara	Princess	Hebrew
Zuri	White or Light skinned	Basque
Zuria	White or Light skinned	Basque
Zurie	White or Light skinned	Basque
BOYS	**MEANING**	**ORIGIN**
Abel	Breath	Hebrew
Acel	Adherent of a nobleman	Unknown
Adrien	Dark	Latin
Advent	Born during Advent	Latin
Agrican	From the field	Unknown
Alain	Handsome	French
Albaric	Blond ruler	German
Albert	Noble and bright	German
Aldrich	Old or wise ruler	English

Aldrick	Old or wise counselor	English
Aleron	Winged	Latin
Alexandre	Defender of mankind	French
Alfred	Wise counselor	Old English
Algrenon	Bearded	English
Aloin	Noble friend	Unknown
Aluin	Noble friend	Unknown
Amaud	Power of an eagle	German
Amaury	Name of a count	French
Ambroise	Divine	French
Ames	Friend	French
Amo	Power of an eagle	German
Amou	Eagle wolf	French
Amoux	Eagle wolf	French
Ancil	God's protection	French
Andre	Manly	French
Andy	Manly	Greek
Ansel	God's protection	French
Ansell	God's protection	French
Anselme	Divine protection	French
Antoine	Priceless, inestimable or praiseworthy	French
Aramis	Fictional swordsman	French
Arber	Dealer of herbs	Unknown
Archaimbaud	Bold	German

Archambault	Bold	German
Archard	Powerful	Unknown
Archenhaud	Bold	German
Archer	Bowman	English
Armand	Soldier	German
Arnaud	Powerful Eagle	French
Aron	Lofty or inspired	Hebrew
Artus	Noble	French
Aubin	Fair	Unknown
Aubrey	Bearlike	French
Aubry	Rules with elf-wisdom	German
Audric	Old or wise ruler	English
Augustin	Majestic	Latin
Auhert	Noble	Unknown
Aurelien	Golden	French
Auriville	From the gold town	Unknown
Austen	Venerable or majestic	Latin
Austin	Majestic	Latin
Austyn	Majestic	Latin
Avenall	Lives near the oatfield	Unknown
Aveneil	Lives near the oatfield	Unknown
Avenelle	Lives near the oatfield	Unknown
Avent	Born during Advent	French
Avery	Elf ruler	English
Bailey	Administrator	French
Baptiste	A baptizer	Latin
Barnabe	Son of prophecy	English

Baron	Warrior	German
Barrie	Lives at the barrier	Unknown
Barry	Marksman	Irish
Barthelemy	Farmer	Arabic
Bartlett	Ploughman	Hebrew
Basile	Kingly	French
Bay	Auburn haired	French
Bayard	Auburn haired	English
Baylen	Auburn haired	English
Bayley	Law enforcer or bailiff	Old English
Beal	Handsome	French
Beale	Handsome	French
Beall	Handsome	French
Beau	Handsome	French
Beaufort	From the beautiful fortress	French
Beauvais	From Beauvais	French
Bell	Handsome	French
Bellamy	Beautiful Friend	Latin
Benjamin	Born of the right hand	Hebrew
Benoit	Blessed	French
Bernard	Brave as a bear	German
Bertram	Illustrious	German
Bertrand	Illustrious	German
Bevis	From Beauvais	French
Blais	Stammerer	Latin
Blaisdell	Stammerer	French

Blaise	Stammerer	Latin
Blaize	Stammerer	Latin
Blase	Stammerer	Latin
Blayze	Stammerer	Latin
Blaze	Stammerer	Latin
Boone	Good	Latin
Boyce	Dweller near the wood	French
Brice	Strength or valor	Welsh
Bruce	Woods	French
Brunelle	Brown or dark haired	French
Bruno	Brown	German
Bryant	Virtuous	Irish
Brys	From Brys	French
Buiron	From the cottage	Unknown
Burcet	Fortress	Unknown
Burdett	Unknown	Unknown
Burdette	Unknown	Unknown
Burel	Reddish brown haired	Unknown
Burkett	Fortress	French
Burnell	Reddish brown haired	French
Burrell	Reddish	Unknown
Byron	From the cottage	French
Caine	Gatherer	Hebrew
Campbell	From the beautiful field	Latin
Carel	Strong	French
Carlo	Strong and manly	Italian
Carlos	Manly	Spanish
Carolos	Manly	Greek

Carolus	Strong	Unknown
Carvell	Village on the marsh	French
Cearbhall	Manly	Unknown
Chance	Fortune or a gamble	French
Chandler	Maker or candles	Old English
Chane	Dependable	Swahili, East Africa
Chaney	Oak	French
Chanler	Maker of candles	Old English
Channing	Canon or church official	French
Chapin	Clergyman	French
Chappel	From the chapel	French
Chappell	From the chapel	French
Charles	Manly	English
Charlot	Son of Charlemagne	French
Chaunce	Church official	English
Chauncey	Church official	English
Chauncy	Church official	English
Chayne	Oak	Unknown
Cheney	From the oak wood	Unknown
Cheval	Horseman or knight	French
Chevalier	Horseman or knight	French
Chevell	Horseman or knight	French

Chevy	Horseman or knight	French
Cheyne	Oak hearted	Unknown
Choncey	Fortune or a gamble	English
Christian	Follower of Christ or anointed	Greek
Christien	Follower of Christ or anointed	French
Christofor	Christ bearer	Greek
Christophe	Christ bearer	French
Claude	Lame	Latin
Clement	Merciful	Latin
Clovis	Renowned warrior	German
Colan	Victory of the people	Greek
Colbert	Renowned seafarer	English
Colbey	Dark or dark haired	Old English
Colin	Victory of the people	Greek
Collin	Victory of the people	Greek
Collins	Victory of the people	Greek
Colyn	Victory of the people	Greek
Constant	Constant or steadfast	Latin
Corben	Raven	Latin
Corbett	Raven	Latin
Corbin	Raven	Latin
Corby	Raven	Latin
Corbyn	Raven	Latin

Cort	Courtier or court attendant	English
Cortland	From the court's land	English
Corvin	Raven haired	English
Court	Courtier or court attendant	English
Courtenay	From Courtenay N France	French
Courtland	From the court's land	English
Courtnay	Courtier or court attendant	English
Courtney	Courtier or court attendant	English
Coyan	Modest	French
Coyne	Modest	French
Cretien	Follower of Christ or anointed	French
Curcio	Polite or courteous	Spanish
Curt	Polite or courteous	French
Curtice	Polite or courteous	French
Curtis	Polite or courteous	French
Curtiss	Polite or courteous	French
Cyprien	From Cyprus	French
Cyrano	From Cyrene	Greek
Cyril	Master or Lord	Greek

Dace	Southerner	Irish
Dacey	Southerner	Irish
Dacian	Southerner	Irish
Daine	From Denmark	English
Damien	To tame	Greek
Daniel	God is my judge	Hebrew
Danton	Praise worthy	French
Darcel	From Arcy	French
Darcell	Fortress	French
Darcio	From Arcy	French
Darcy	From Arcy	French
D'Arcy	From Arcy	French
Dareau	Grove of oak tree	French
Dariel	Little darling	French
Dariell	Little darling	French
Darrell	Darling	French
Darroll	Darling	French
Dartagnan	Unknown	French
Darvell	Town of eagles	French
Davet	Beloved	French
David	Beloved	Hebrew
Davin	Brilliant Finn	Scandinavian
Dax	Water	French
Dayne	From Denmark	Scandinavian
Del	Proud friend	English
Delaine	Son of the challenger	Irish
Delancy	Son of the challenger	Irish
Delane	Son of the challenger	Irish
Delaney	Son of the challenger	Irish

Delano	Nut tree	French
Delmar	Of the sea	Latin
Delmer	Of the sea	Latin
Delmon	Of the mountain	English
Delmont	Of the mountain	English
Delmore	Of the sea	Latin
Delray	Belonging to the King	French
Delrick	Belonging to the King	Unknown
Delrico	Belonging to the King	Unknown
Delron	Belonging to the King	Unknown
Delroy	Belonging to the King	French
Denis	God of wine	French
Dennet	God of wine	Greek
Dennis	God of wine	Greek
Denver	Green valley	English
Denys	God of wine	French
Deon	God of wine	Greek
Derell	Darling or beloved	French
Derrall	Darling or beloved	French
Derrell	Darling or beloved	French
Derrill	Darling or beloved	French
Desire	Desired or longed for	English
Destan	By the still waters	Unknown
Destin	Fate	French
Deston	Fate	French
Destrey	Fate	American

Destrie	Fate	American
Destry	Fate	American
Deveral	Riverbank	English
Devere	Riverbank	English
Devereau	Riverbank	French
Devereaux	Riverbank	French
Deverel	Riverbank	English
Deverell	Riverbank	English
Deverick	Riverbank	English
Devery	Riverbank	English
Devin	Poet	Irish
Devry	Riverbank	English
Diandre	Manly	French
Didier	Desired or longed for	French
Dilan	Faithful or loyal	Irish
Dillen	Faithful or loyal	Irish
Dillon	Faithful or loyal	Irish
Dimitri	Of the earth	Greek
Dion	God of wine	Greek
Diondre	Manly	French
Dionte	God of wine	Greek
Dix	Tenth	French
Dominique	Belonging to the Lord	French
Donatien	Gift of God	French
Dondre	God of wine	French
Drago	Dragon	Italian
Dru	Manly	English
Dumont	Of the mountain	Unknown
Duran	Firm or enduring	Latin
Durand	Firm or enduring	Latin

Durango	Strong	Latin
Durant	Firm or enduring	Latin
Durante	Firm or enduring	Latin
Dureau	Strong	French
Duron	Strong	Latin
Durrant	Firm or enduring	Latin
Duval	Of the valley	French
Edgard	Lucky spearman	French
Edmon	Prosperous protector	Old English
Edmond	Prosperous protector	Old English
Edmund	Prosperous protector	Old English
Edmundo	Prosperous protector	Spanish
Edouard	Wealthy guardian	French
Eduard	Wealthy guardian	German
Eliot	Jehovah is God	French
Eliott	Jehovah is God	French
Elliot	Jehovah is God	French
Eloy	Chosen one	Latin
Emile	Industrious	French
Eric	Eternal ruler	Scandinavian
Eriq	Eternal ruler	French
Ernest	Sincere	English
Etienne	Crowned	French
Eugene	Well born or noble	French
Fabien	Bean grower	French

Fabrice	Craftsman	French
Felix	Fortunate or happy	Latin
Fernand	Adventurer	German
Firman	Firm or strong	French
Fitz	Son of	English
Fitzgerald	Son of Gerald	English
Fitzhugh	Son of Hugh	English
Fitzpatrick	Son of Patrick	English
Fletcher	Arrow maker	Old English
Florentin	Blooming or flowering	French
Florian	Blooming or flowering	Latin
Florus	Flower	Latin
Fontaine	Fountain	French
Fontane	Fountain	French
Fontayne	Fountain	French
Fonteyne	Fountain	French
Forrest	Woodsman	French
Fortun	Fortunate or lucky	French
Fortune	Fortunate or lucky	French
Francois	Free or from France	French
Frank	Free or from France	English
Frankie	Free or from France	English
Franky	Free or from France	English
Frederic	Peaceful ruler	French
Freman	Free man	English
Fremont	Noble protector	German
Gace	Pledge	Unknown

Gaetan	Fom Gaete	Italian
Garan	Guards or guardian	English
Gard	Keeper of the garden	English
Gardiner	Keeper of the garden	English
Gardner	Keeper of the garden	English
Garen	Mighty with a spear	English
Garin	Mighty with a spear	English
Garion	Mighty with a spear	English
Garlan	Wreath or prize	French
Garland	Wreath or prize	French
Garlen	Wreath or prize	French
Garlyn	Wreath or prize	French
Garnell	Keeper of grain	French
Garner	Sentry	French
Garnet	Pomegranate seed	English
Garon	Mighty with a spear	English
Garren	Mighty with a spear	English
Garrin	Mighty with a spear	English
Garron	Mighty with a spear	English
Gascon	From Gascony	French
Gaspar	Treasurer	French

Gaspard	Treasurer	French
Gaston	From Gascony	French
Gaston	From Gascony	French
Gauthier	Woodsman	French
Gautier	Woodsman	French
Geffrey	Peaceful	English
Geoff	Peaceful	English
Geoffrey	Peaceful	English
Geoffroy	Peaceful	French
Georges	Farmer	French
Gerald	Mighty with a spear	German
Gerard	Brave with a spear	Old English
Germain	From Germany	French
Germano	German	Italian
Geron	Mighty with a spear	English
Gerrard	Brave with a spear	English
Gifford	Gift of bravery	Old English
Gil	Shield bearer	Greek
Gilbert	Illustrious pledge	English
Gill	Trustworthy	English
Gilles	Shield bearer	French
Granville	Large town	French
Gregoire	Vigilant watchman	French
Grenville	Large village	French
Grosvenor	Great hunter	French
Guifford	Bold giver	English
Guillaume	Resolute protector	French

Gustav	Staff of the Goths	Old Norse
Gustave	Staff of the Goths	Scandinavian
Guy	Guide	French
Hamilton	Proud home	English
Harbin	Glorious warrior	German
Harcourt	Fortified dwelling	French
Hardouin	Name of a count	French
Harman	Noble	Latin
Harmen	Noble	Latin
Harmon	Noble	Latin
Henri	Ruler of the enclosure	French
Henry	Ruler of the enclosure	German
Herbert	Illustrious warrior	German
Herve	Army warrior	French
Hubert	Bright mind	German
Hugh	Bright mind	English
Hyacinthe	Hyacinth	Greek
Ignace	Fiery or ardent	French
Isaak	Laughter	Hebrew
Isidore	Gift of Isis	Greek
Iven	Little archer	French
Jacquelin	Supplanter	French
Jacques	Supplanter	French
Jaques	Supplanter	French
Jasper	Treasurer	French
Javier	Owner of a new house	Spanish
Jay	Blue jay	French
Jaye	Blue jay	French

234

Jean	God is gracious	French
Jean Baptiste	French form of John the Baptist	French
Jeffrey	Divinely peaceful	Old English
Jeoffroi	Divinely peaceful	French
Jerard	Mighty with a spear	French
Jeremie	God will uplift	English
Jerome	Holy name	Latin
Jesper	Jasperstone	French
Jocelyn	Joyous	Latin
Joel	God is willing	Hebrew
Johnn	God is gracious	Hebrew
Johnnie	God is gracious	Hebrew
Johnny	God is gracious	Hebrew
John-paul	Gift of God and small	Hebrew
Johnson	Son of John	Old English
Jolie	Pretty	French
Jon	God is gracious	Hebrew
Jonn	God is gracious	Hebrew
Jonnie	God is gracious	Hebrew
Jorden	To flow down or descend	Hebrew
Jordon	To flow down or descend	Hebrew
Joseph	God will add	Hebrew

Jourdan	To flow down or descend	French
Joy	Rejoicing	Latin
Jules	Downy bearded or youthful	French
Julian	Downy bearded or youthful	Latin
Julien	Downy bearded or youthful	Latin
Julius	Downy bearded or youthful	Latin
Jullien	Downy bearded or youthful	Latin
Justin	Just	Latin
Kaarle	Strong and manly	Unknown
Kaarlo	Strong and manly	Unknown
Kalle	Strong and manly	Scandinavian
Kalman	Strong and manly	Unknown
Karcsi	Strong and manly	Unknown
Karel	Strong and manly	Slovak
Kari	Pure	Greek
Karl	Farmer	German
Karlens	Strong and manly	Russian
Karlis	Strong and manly	Russian
Karlitis	Strong and manly	Unknown

Karoly	Strong and manly	Slavic
Kerman	From Germany	Basque
Lafayette	French nobleman	French
Lamar	Of the sea	French
Lamarr	Of the sea	French
Lance	Attendant	German
Lancelin	Attendant	French
Lancelot	Attendant	French
Landers	Landowner	English
Landis	Landowner	English
Landry	Ruler	Old English
Langley	From the long meadow	Old English
L'Angley	Englishman	Unknown
Laramie	Tears of happiness	French
Larue	The red haired one	French
Lasalle	The hall	French
Latimer	Interpreter	English
Launcelot	Attendant	French
Laurent	Crowned with laurels	French
Leal	Faithful or loyal	French
Leandre	Lion man or brave as a lion	French
Leeroy	The king	French
Legget	Delegate	French
Lenard	Brave as a lion	German
Lennard	Brave as a lion	German
Leo	Lion	Latin

Name	Meaning	Origin
Leocadie	Brave as a lion	Unknown
Leodegrance	Brave as a lion	French
Leon	Brave as a lion	German
Leonard	Brave as a lion	German
Leonce	Brave as a lion	French
Leone	Brave as a lion	Italian
Leonore	Light	Greek
Leroi	The king	French
Leron	The circle	French
Leroux	The red haired one	French
Leroy	The king	French
Leveret	Young rabbit	French
Leverett	Young rabbit	French
Lionel	Young lion	French
Lionell	Young lion	French
Lisle	From the island	Unknown
Lonell	Young lion	English
Lonnell	Young lion	English
Loring	From Lorraine	French
Lothair	Famous warrior	German
Louis	Famous warrior	German
Louvel	Little wolf	French
Lovell	Young wolf	French
Lowe	Little wolf	French
Lowell	Young wolf	French
Loyal	Faithful	English
Luc	Bringer of	French

	light	
Lucian	Bringer of light	Latin
Lucien	Bringer of light	French
Lyle	From the island	French
Madelon	From the high tower	French
Mahieu	Gift of God	French
Mailhairer	Ill fated	Unknown
Malleville	From Malleville	Unknown
Mallory	Army counselor	German
Mandel	Almond	German
Manneville	Workers village	French
Mantel	Makes garments	Unknown
Manville	Workers village	French
Marc	Warlike	French
Marceau	Warlike	French
Marcel	Warlike	French
Marius	Warlike	Latin
Markey	Warlike	Latin
Marlon	Falcon	French
Marmion	Small one	French
Marq	Warlike	French
Marque	Warlike	French
Marquis	Nobleman	French
Marsh	Steward of horses	French
Marshal	Steward of horses	French
Marshall	Steward of horses	French

Maslin	Little Thomas	French
Mason	Stone worker	French
Masselin	Little Thomas	French
Masson	Stone worker	French
Mathieu	Gift of God	French
Matthieu	Gift from God	French
Maurice	Dark skinned	Latin
Maxime	Most excellent	French
Mayhew	Gift of God	English
Maynard	Powerful	English
Mayne	Powerful	English
Maynor	Powerful	English
Melville	Mill town	French
Mercer	Merchant	English
Merle	Falcon	French
Merlin	Falcon	Celtic
Merlion	Falcon	Unknown
Michel	Who is like God	French
Michele	Who is like God	French
Mikel	Who is like God	Basque
Millard	Caretaker of the mill	Latin
Miquel	Who is like God	Spanish
Montague	Pointed mountain	French
Montaigu	Pointed mountain	French
Montaine	Mountain	French
Montgomery	Rich man's mountain	Old English
Moor	Marshland	French
Moore	Marshland	French
More	Marshland	French

240

Morell	Dark one or the Moor	French
Nacisse	Daffodil	Latin
Nann	Favor or grace	Unknown
Napoleon	Lion of the woodland	Greek
Nathalia	Birthday of Christ	Russian
Nathanael	God has given	Hebrew
Navarre	Plains	French
Neuveville	From the new town	French
Neville	New village	French
Nichol	Victory of the people	French
Nicolas	Victory of the people	Greek
Noe	Rest or comfort	French
Noel	Christmas	French
Noell	Christmas	French
Noreis	Caretaker	Unknown
Norice	Caretaker	Unknown
Norm	From the north	French
Norman	From the north	French
Normand	From the north	French
Norris	Northerner	French
Nouel	Unknown	French
Octave	Born eighth	French
Odo	Rich	Scandinavian
Oliver	Olive tree	Latin
Olivier	From the olive tree	French
Onfroi	Peaceful Hun	French

ONille	From the gold town	Irish
Orson	Bear like	Latin
Orvelle	Golden village	French
Orvil	Golden village	French
Orville	Golden village	French
Ourson	Little bear	Unknown
Padgett	Attendant	English
Page	Attendant	French
Paget	Attendant	French
Paien	Name of a nobleman	French
Paige	Attendant	French
Parfait	Perfect	French
Paris	Lover	Greek
Pascal	Born on Easter	French
Pascual	Born on Easter	Spanish
Pasquale	Born at Easter	Italian
Patric	Nobleman	Latin
Patrice	Noble	French
Paul	Small	Latin
Paulin	Small	Latin
Pepperell	Piper	Unknown
Peppin	Petitioner	German
Perceval	Pierces	French
Percival	Pierces	French
Percy	Pierces	French
Perren	Rock	French
Perrin	Rock	French
Perry	Rock	French
Perryn	Rock	French
Peverell	Piper	French

Philip	Lover of horses	Latin
Philippe	Lover of horses	French
Phillipe	Lover of horses	French
Pierpont	Rock	French
Pierre	Rock	French
Pierrepont	Rock	French
Piers	Lover of horses	French
Piperel	Piper	French
Pippin	Father	German
Plat	Flat land	French
Platt	Flat land	French
Pomeroy	Apple orchard	French
Pommelraie	Apple orchard	French
Porter	Gatekeeper	Latin
Porteur	Gatekeeper	French
Portier	Gatekeeper	French
Preruet	Brave little one	French
Prewitt	Brave little one	French
Priour	Head of a monastery	French
Prosper	Fortunite	Latin
Pruet	Brave little one	French
Pruie	Brave little one	French
Pruitt	Brave little one	French
Pryor	Head of a monastery	Latin
Quennel	From the little oak tree	French

243

Quent	Fifth	Latin
Quentin	Fifth	Latin
Quenton	Fifth	Latin
Quentrell	Fifth	Latin
Quesnel	From the little oak tree	French
Quincey	Fifth	French
Quincy	Fifth	French
Quint	Fifth	Latin
Quinton	Fifth	Latin
Quintrell	Fifth	Latin
Raimond	Wise protector	German
Raimundo	Wise protector	Spanish
Rainger	Ward of the forest	Unknown
Rainier	Strong counselor	French
Ramond	Wise protector	English
Ranger	Ward of the forest	French
Ranier	Strong counselor	French
Raoul	Wolf counsel	French
Ray	Regal	French
Rayce	Counselor	Unknown
Rayder	Counselor	Unknown
Raydon	Counselor	Unknown
Rayford	Counselor	English
Raylen	Counselor	English
Raymond	Wise protector	English
Raymund	Wise protector	English
Raymundo	Wise protector	Spanish

Raynard	Strong counselor	French
Raynell	Counselor	English
Remi	Rower	French
Remy	Rower	French
Renard	Strong counselor	French
Renaud	Wise power	French
Rene	Reborn	French
Renne	Small but strong	Irish
Rennie	Small but strong	Irish
Renny	Small but strong	Irish
Reule	Famous wolf	French
Reve	Dream	Unknown
Rey	Regal	Spanish
Reymond	Wise protector	English
Reymundo	Wise protector	Spanish
Reynard	Strong counselor	French
Ricard	Rich and powerful ruler	French
Richard	Rich and powerful ruler	English
Richardo	Rich and powerful ruler	Spanish
Rique	Rich and powerful ruler	French
Rob	Bright with fame	English
Robb	Bright with	English

	fame	
Robbie	Bright with fame	English
Robby	Bright with fame	English
Robert	Bright with fame	English
Roch	Rock	French
Roche	Rock	French
Rocke	Rock	French
Rodel	Famous ruler	Unknown
Rodell	Famous ruler	Unknown
Roel	Rock	Unknown
Roi	King	French
Roland	Famous in the land	German
Rolando	Famous in the land	Spanish
Rollan	Famous in the land	German
Rolland	Famous in the land	German
Rollie	Famous in the land	German
Rollo	Famous in the land	German
Romain	A Roman	French
Roselin	Red haired	French
Roselyn	Red haired	French
Rosiyn	Red haired	French
Roslin	Red haired	French
Rosselin	Red haired	French
Rosselyn	Red haired	French
Rousse	Red haired	French
Roussel	Reddish	French
Rousset	Red haired	French
Rousskin	Red haired	Unknown
Rowland	Famous in	German

	the land	
Roy	King	French
Royal	Regal	French
Royce	Kingly	French
Royden	From the rye hill	English
Ruelle	Famous wolf	French
Ruff	Red haired	French
Ruffe	Red haired	French
Rui	Regal	French
Rule	Famous wolf	French
Rush	Red haired	French
Rushe	Red haired	French
Rushkin	Red haired	French
Russ	Red haired	French
Russel	Red haired	French
Russell	Red haired	French
Rust	Red haired	French
Saber	Sword	French
Sage	Wise	Latin
Samuel	Heard by God	Hebrew
Sargent	A squire	French
Satordi	Saturn	French
Saul	Longed for	Hebrew
Sauville	Willow town	French
Saville	Willow town	French
Searlas	Manly	Irish
Searle	Armor	English
Searlus	Manly	Irish
Sebastien	Revered	French
Seignour	Lord of the manor	French
Senet	Elderly	French
Senior	Lord of the manor	French
Sennet	Elderly	French
Serge	Attendant	Latin

Severin	Severe	French
Sevrin	Severe	French
Seymour	Prayer	French
Sid	From St. Denys	French
Sidney	From St. Denys	French
Silvestre	Forest dweller	French
Simon	God is heard	Hebrew
Sinclair	Prayer	French
Sinclaire	Prayer	French
Sinjin	Holyman	English
Somer	Bom in summer	Unknown
Somerville	Summer town	English
Sorel	Reddish brown hair	French
Soren	Thunder	Danish
Sorrell	Reddish brown hair	French
Stephan	Crown or wreath	Greek
Stephane	Crown	Latin
Sumarville	Summer town	English
Sumner	Summoner	English
Syd	From St. Denys	French
Sydney	Wide meadow	French
Sylvain	Forest	Latin
Sylvestre	Of the forest	Latin
Taillefer	Works in iron	French
Talbot	Boot maker	French
Talehot	Bloodhound	Unknown
Talon	Claw	English

Name	Meaning	Origin
Tanguy	Warrior	Celtic
Tavin	Royal staff	Scandinavian
Taylor	Tailor	English
Tearlach	Manly	Scottish
Telfer	Works with iron	French
Telfor	Works with iron	French
Telford	Works with iron	French
Telfour	Works with iron	French
Theon	Untamed	Unknown
Theron	Hunter	Greek
Therron	Hunter	Greek
Thibaud	People's prince	French
Thibault	Prince of the people	German
Thieny	Rule of the people	French
Thierry	Ruler of the people	French
Thomas	Twin	Greek
Tibault	Ruler of the people	French
Toussnint	All saints	French
Trace	Harvester	Greek
Tracy	Harvester	Greek
Travers	From the crossroads	French
Travis	Crossroads	English
Treves	Crossroads	English
Tristan	Bold	Welsh
Tristen	Bold	Welsh
Tristian	Bold	French
Tristin	Bold	Welsh
Troy	Foot soldier	Irish

Troyes	Curly haired	French
Turner	Lathe worker	Latin
Tyce	Fiery	French
Tyeis	Son of a German	French
Tyeson	Fiery	French
Tyson	Firebrand	French
Ulrich	World ruler	German
Urbain	City dweller or from the city	Latin
Vachel	Little cow	French
Vail	Valley	English
Valentin	Strong	Latin
Valiant	Brave	Latin
Vallis	A Welshman	French
Vallois	A Welshman	French
Vardan	From the green hill	French
Varden	From the green hill	French
Vardon	From the green hill	French
Vayle	Valley	French
Verddun	From the green hill	French
Verdell	Green or flourishing	French
Verel	Correct	French
Vern	Youthful or springlike	Latin
Vernay	Springlike	Latin
Verne	Youthful or springlike	Latin
Vernell	Springlike	Latin
Verney	From the alder grove	French

Vernon	Youthful or springlike	Latin
Verrall	Manly	German
Verrell	Manly	German
Verrill	Manly	German
Veryl	Manly	German
Vic	Conqueror	Latin
Vick	Conqueror	Latin
Vicq	Conqueror	Latin
Victor	Conqueror	Latin
Vidal	Life	French
Videl	Life	French
Vincent	Conquering	Latin
Warrane	Warden of the game	French
Wiatt	Little warrior	French
William	Resolute protector	German
Wyatt	Little warrior	French
Xarles	Manly	French
Yves	Archer	French
Yvet	Archer	French
Yvon	Archer	French
Zdenek	Follower of Saint Denys	Slovak

Unisex

In a world where more and more people are breaking out of the molds put in place by gender, parents are opting to go for unisex names. These names can be for a boy or a girl – or anyone in between. Some of names you'll hear on an everyday basis, like Aubrey, and others you won't hear all that often. This is also a great way to name your baby if you are keeping the sex a surprise!

BOY OR GIRL	MEANING	ORIGIN
Addison	Son of Adam	English
Adrian	Dark	Latin
Alex	Defender of mankind	Greek
Alexis	Defender of mankind	Greek
Andy	Manly	Greek
Angel	Messenger	Latin
Ariel	Lion of God	Hebrew
Arron	Enlightened	Hebrew
Ashley	Meadow of ash trees	Old English
Ashton	Ash tree enclosure	Old English
Aubrey	Bearlike or blond ruler	French
Avery	Elf ruler	English
Baby	Infant	English
Bailey	Administrator	French
Billy	Resolute protector	German
Blaine	Slender or thin	Irish
Blair	Dweller on the plain	Scottish
Brett	From Britain	Irish
Brice	Swift	Irish
Caden	Barrel	English
Cameron	Crooked nose	Scottish
Carmen	Song	Latin
Carmine	Song	Latin

Carson	Son of Carr	Old English
Cary	Descendant of the dark one	Welsh
Casey	Brave	Irish
Cassidy	Clever or curly headed	Irish
Cecil	Dim sighted or blind	Latin
Chandler	Maker of candles	Old English
Christian	Follower of Christ or anointed	Greek
Cody	Cushion	Old English
Connor	Exalted/wise/constant	Irish/Scottish/Latin
Corey	Dweller near a hollow	Irish
Cullen	Handsome	Irish
Dakota	Allies or friends	Sioux
Dallas	Waterfall near the field	Scottish
Dana	From Denmark	Old Norse
Dane	From Denmark	Old English
Darren	Great	Irish
Darryl	Darling	French
Delaney	Son of the challenger	Irish
Devon	Poet	Irish
Donovan	Dark warrior	Irish
Drew	Manly	English
Duncan	Brown warrior	Scottish
Dustin	Valiant fighter	German
Dylan	Son of the sea	Welsh
Elisha	God is my salvation	Hebrew
Ellery	From the elder tree island	English
Emerson	Industrious ruler	German
Erin	Ireland	Irish
Evan	Youth warrior	Irish
Fabian	Bean grower	Latin
Florian	Blooming or flowering	Latin
Francis	Free or from France	Latin

Glen	Secluded valley or glen	Irish
Hadley	From the heather covered meadow	Old English
Haiden	From the hedged valley	English
Harley	From the hare's meadow	English
Hayden	From the hedged valley	English
Hayley	From the hay meadow	English
Hunter	A huntsman	English
Ira	Watchful or vigilant	Hebrew
Israel	Contender with God	Hebrew
Jade	Stone of the side	Spanish
Jaden	Stone of the side	English
James	Supplanter	English
Jamie	Supplanter	English
Jan	God is gracious	Scandinavian
Jerry	Mighty spearman	German
Jesse	Wealthy	Hebrew
Jordan	To flow down or descend	Hebrew
Jude	Praised	Hebrew
Julian	Downy bearded or youthful	Latin
Justice	Just	Latin
Kadin	Companion	Arabic
Kelly	Warrior	Irish
Kelsey	Ship island	Scottish
Kendall	Valley of the river Kent	Old English
Kennedy	Ugly head	Irish
Kerry	Dark haired one	Irish
Kiley	Land where cattle graze or beautiful	Irish

Kimberley	Fortress meadow	Old English
Lane	A narrow country road	Old English
Lee	Dweller near the wood or clearing	Old English
Leslie	From the gray fortress	Scottish
Lindsay	Island of linden trees	Old English
Logan	Dweller in a little hollow	Irish
London	Fortress	Old English
Lonnie	Ready for battle	German
Lucian	Bringer of light	Latin
MacKenzie	Fair one or handsome	Irish
Madison	Mighty in battle	English
Mallory	Unfortunate or unlucky	French
Marley	From the lake meadow	English
Mason	Stone worker	French
McKenna	Ascend	Gaelic
Meredith	Protector of the sea	Welsh
Michael	Who is like God	Hebrew
Montana	Mountainous	Spanish
Morgan	Bright Sea	Welsh
Moriah	Jehovah is my teacher	Hebrew
Nevada	Snowy	Spanish
Noel	Christmas	French
Orion	Son of fire	Greek
Paris	Lover	Greek
Parker	Gamekeeper	English
Payton	A town or settlement	Old English
Perry	Dweller by the pear tree	English
Quinn	Fifth	Irish
Raphael	God has healed	Hebrew
Ravenel	Raven	English
Reagan	Little king	Irish

Reed	Redheaded	English
Reese	Ardor	Welsh
Regan	Little ruler	Irish
Rene	Reborn	French
Riley	Dweller by the rye field	Old English
Robin	Bright fame	English
Ryan	Little king	Irish
Sage	Wise	Latin
Scout	To observe or to spy	English
Sean	God is gracious	Irish
Shane	God is gracious	Irish
Shay	Supplanter	Irish
Shelby	Village on the ledge	English
Silver	Lustrous	Old English
Skye	The isle of Skye	Scottish
Skylar	The isle of Skye	Scottish
Sonny	A young boy	English
Spencer	Dispenser of provisions	Old English
Stacy	Resurrection	Russian
Stormy	Tempestuous	English
Sunny	Bright or cheerful	English
Sydney	Wide meadow	French
Taylor	To cut	French
Terry	Smooth	Latin
Tony	Worthy of praise	Latin
Tory	Victory	Old English
Tracy	Harvester	Greek
Tyler	Tile maker	French
Tyne	A river in England	Old English
Wallace	From Wales	English
Wesley	A clearing in the west	Old English
Whitney	White island	Old English
Wynne	Fair or white	English
Zane	Gift of God	English

Made in the USA
Lexington, KY
08 January 2019